Alfred Duquet

Ireland and France

Alfred Duquet

Ireland and France

ISBN/EAN: 9783741188978

Manufactured in Europe, USA, Canada, Australia, Japa

Cover: Foto ©ninafisch / pixelio.de

Manufactured and distributed by brebook publishing software (www.brebook.com)

Alfred Duquet

Ireland and France

Août 1871.

IRELAND AND FRANCE.

FROM THE FRENCH OF

ALFRED DUQUET.

WITH A SKETCH OF THE LIFE OF

MARSHAL MacMAHON,

Second President of the French Republic.

BALTIMORE:
JOHN MURPHY COMPANY.
1899.

TO THE

FAST AND FIRM FRIEND AND CHAMPION OF THE
IRISH RACE

PATRICK FORD, Esq.
Editor *Irish World*, New York

THIS LITTLE VOLUME IS RESPECTFULLY DEDICATED BY
THE TRANSLATOR.

CONTENTS.

CHAPTER.		PAGE.
I.	The Red Cross Society—Prussians violated neutrality laws—Sympathy for France.................	11
II.	Irish Brigade and the Ambulance Relief Corps land at Havre—English Relief Corps lands also at Havre..	13
III.	Ambulance Corps on the battlefield—The Student and the Black Charger.........................	17
IV.	Visit to England by the French Delegation—Another Delegation sets out for Ireland.........	19
V.	From Paris to London......................................	21
VI.	From London to Holyhead.............................	23
VII.	Arrival at Kingstown—"*Cead-mille-failthe*" for the French Delegates...................................	25
VIII.	From Kingstown to Dublin—A grand ovation....	27
IX.	In Dublin—Breakfast at Mr. Lombard's—Grand Meeting and Banquet—Franco-Irish Ambulance—The O'Neills of Tyrone—Letters from the Archbishop of Orleans and President MacMahon—No Home Rule for Ireland—The French and Irish workingmen—The Republic—Welcome for the French—Reply of Viscount de Flavigney, president of the Delegation—Eloquent speech of Mr. A. M. Sullivan—Reply of Mr. Ferdinand de Lesseps.........................	28
X.	Address by the Municipality of Dublin to the French Delegates—Sightseeing through the city—Dinner at the Lord Lieutenant's...........	46

CONTENTS.

CHAPTER.		PAGE.
XI.	Excursion to the Co. Wicklow—Powerscourt Waterfall—Vartry Waterworks—At Glendalough, and the "Meeting of the Waters"—Visit to Father Fox's Orphan Asylum.......	52
XII.	Visit to Mallow and Cork—Great Demonstrations at Marleborough, Thurles and Limerick Junction—Arrival at Mallow, Blarney and Cork—The Lord Mayor of Cork presents an address—Count de Flavigney replies and thanks all Ireland in the name of France for the assistance given during the war—Addresses of the workingmens' club, and a delegation from Youghall—Speech of Mr. John Martin—Visit to Queenstown—On board the man-of-war Northumberland, Captain Gibbons commanding—Dinner and speechmaking at Ashgrove—O'Neill of Tyrone and the Duke de Feltre make speeches...........	57
XIII.	From Cork to Glengarriffe—Arrival at Macroom—Lunch at the beautiful lake called Gougane Barra—Visit to island ruins of St. Finbar—J. J. Callanan's description of it—Bantry Bay—The French invasion—The winds save England—Fiat Lux.......	69
XIV.	From Glengarriffe to Killarney—O'Sullivan's march—Tunnel through the mountain like that of St. Gervais of Chamony—Arrival at Kenmare—Visit to Catholic Church and Convent School........	75
XV.	At Killarney—Ovation to the French Delegates—France was beaten because she was unprepared for war—Visit to the Lakes—Mucross Abbey—O'Sullivan's Cascade—Innisfallen......	78
XVI.	Killarney to Dublin—Orange bigotry—Viscount de Flavigney, President of the French Delega-	

CONTENTS.

CHAPTER.		PAGE.
	tion, charmed the Irish people—The Foresters—Dinner at the Mansion House—Viscount O'Neill of Tyrone and the Irish Brigade.........	84
XVII.	Mass at the Jesuits' Church—Eloquent sermon by Father Bannon, on "France the Queen of civilization, and the Protector of all oppressed nations"—Departure of the French Delegates—A grand send-off...	91
XVIII.	From Dublin to London—In London—Beware of pickpockets..	94
XIX.	From London to Paris—Arrival at Versailles—Marshal MacMahon well pleased with our reception in Ireland..	96
XX.	Conclusion—Thanks to Ireland.......................	98
XXI.	Treaty of Geneva..	100

APPENDIX.

MARSHAL MACMAHON, SECOND PRESIDENT OF THE FRENCH REPUBLIC.

I. The grandfather of MacMahon was a native of Limerick, Ireland—MacMahon was born June 13, 1808, at the Castle of Sully—At 17 he entered the school of St. Cyr, and graduated in 1827—Lieutenant of the 4th Hussars in 1830—Went to Algiers in '31—Then received the Cross of the Legion of Honor—Afterwards appointed Colonel of the 41st Regiment of the line....................... 109

II. MacMahon was made General of Brigade in '48, and in '52 Military Governor of Constantinople, and General of division afterwards.................... 112

CONTENTS.

		PAGE
III.	The Crimean War—On September 8th, 1855, the Malakoff, the key of Sebastopol was taken by MacMahon, for which he was named Senator of France	112
IV.	War with Austria—MacMahon gains a great victory—Created Marshal and Duke of Magenta	114
V.	Franco-Prussian War—MacMahon's plans not heeded—Battle of Woerth, Metz, and Sedan—MacMahon wounded and taken prisoner	115
VI.	MacMahon and the Commune	117
VII.	MacMahon elected President of the French Republic—He is superior to the greed of office—Retired in 1879—He died in October, 1893	119

PREFACE.

The terrible slaughter of the Commune is at an end. Our conquered army has returned home. Alsace and Lorraine are now German territory. In fine, the war is over, thanks be to the Lord.

Notwithstanding all our misfortunes, it is pleasant to know that there was one people who did not abandon us in our trials. One people who has the same esteem for us now, as it had before the war; and that is the Irish people.

In this little volume, we shall briefly relate a few facts about the French and Irish Red Cross Societies during the late war between France and Prussia. The good these societies have done for the poor wounded soldiers; and also the grand ovations which the Irish people gave to the French delegates on their recent visit to Ireland. Let it be understood that the opinions here expressed, are our own personally.

IRELAND AND FRANCE.

CHAPTER I.

THE RED CROSS SOCIETY.

THE French Red Cross Society was formed recently to relieve all sick and wounded soldiers. It is one of the blessed works which do honor to our common humanity. It is fraternal charity carried to its utmost limit, because it makes no distinction between friend and foe. The ambulances and military hospitals were made neutral by the Geneva convention, and this condition affected physicians, chaplains, nurses and ambulance corps. (See Treaty of Geneva, below.)

THE PRUSSIANS VIOLATED NEUTRALITY LAWS.

Being taken prisoners in September, we saw at Versailles and at Rambouillet, a number of Prussian soldiers wearing the Red Cross, and armed to the teeth at the same time. We inquired the reason why they acted so. "Oh!" they said, "we shoot first, and then we gather up the wounded."

SYMPATHY FOR FRANCE.

The sympathy manifested for France by the Irish people during the Franco-Prussian war, was very deep and very emphatically pronounced indeed. After the defeat of the French army at Woerth, at Forback, and at Sedan, a gloom of sorrow was cast over all Ireland, because her friend and ally emerged from the fray non-victorious.

CHAPTER II.

THE IRISH BRIGADE AND AMBULANCE RELIEF SOCIETY.

AT a meeting called by the leading men of Dublin, in September 1870, an ambulance corps was formed, and dispatched to France immediately with money, linen and medicine.

Mr. P. J. Smith was sent to France to communicate with the French Government. The Ambulance, which consisted of 300 persons, 10 horses and 5 wagons, was a godsend, and was received by the French with open arms. In more ways than one did Ireland help France in the hour of her need, and during the war the Irish heart went out in sympathy to her. A brigade was formed at Caen, consisting of 600 men, all Irish; this little army fought bravely on the plains of Beauce and Franche-Comte; and Captain Kirwan distinguished himself for his bravery during the campaign.

LANDING OF THE IRISH AMBULANCE RELIEF
CORPS AT HAVRE. OCTOBER 13, 1870.

The Ambulance Relief Corps, which arrived from Ireland by the steamer La Fontaine, was officially received this morning. From an early hour the streets of the city were thronged with people. Two battalions of artillery of the national guard, one company of marines, three companies of la garde-nationale, a detachment of troops of the line, with their commanders, formed upon the boulevard-de-Strasbourg. At 9.30 the order to march was given. Whilst the line passed the headquarters of the Ambulance Corps, there was a continual cheer of "Vive l'Irlande! Vive la France!" After the arrival of the city officials, Mr. Alfred Duquet stepped forward and said:—

"*Gentlemen:* Viscount de Flavigney has appointed me to receive you, upon the soil of our dear country, in the name of the French International Ambulance Relief Society. It is needless to express to you, how much our unhappy country is touched, with the sympathy shown us by Ireland, in the moment of our affliction. 'A friend in need is a friend indeed.' Gentlemen, in the name of our country, you are a thousand times welcome."

Mr. Sigfried spoke for the city, as follows:—

"*Gentlemen:* The city of Havre: the people of the city of Havre are happy to be able to extend to you a Caed-Mille-Failthe. We are delighted to be able to acknowledge our gratitude for the good work you have come to do amongst us. It is a hard and difficult task, and the only recompense you will have, is the thought of having done nobly;

the gratitude of the wounded soldiers and the heartfelt thanks of the French people: 'God save Ireland.'"

Then Colonel Massu made a nice little speech, in the name of the French army. Mr. McCann, one of the Aldermen of Dublin, replied as follows:—

"On the part of a sister nation, a nation intimately united with France by innumerable historical alliances, I present to you delegates of the noble French nation, this Ambulance Relief Corps. If it can render you any assistance in this hour of your trial, it shall have accomplished the mission very dear to the Irish people."

After the applause had subsided, Mr. P. J. Smith, M. P. for the Co. Dublin, spoke very eloquently and with much warmth, as follows:—

"*Gentlemen:* Permit me to extend to you the assurance of the most tender sympathies of the sons and daughters of Ireland. We wish to be separated from the shameful indifference of the rest of Europe. We are Irishmen, and as Irishmen we declare our friendship in the cause of France. Ireland is with France to-day as she has always been, and if Ireland could, she would send her sons to fight, and if need be, to die for France." (Great applause greeted every sentence).

At a given signal, the line of march was taken up, and the procession continued on to the Hotel-de-Ville. Every soldier wore a green ribbon, and as the green flag passed along, nothing could be heard but "Vive l'Irlande! Vive l'Irlande! Vive l'Irlande!" The Ambulance Relief Corps was received in the court of the Hotel-de-Ville, after which a magnificent repast was served. During the dinner many national airs were played. Our Irish friends surely must have noticed how much their services were appreciated by us.

The English sent an Ambulance Relief Corps to the Prussians. They crossed the channel, and landed also at Havre, some time after the Irish. At Havre, the authorities and the people of that city gave the English a grand reception.

CHAPTER III.

THE AMBULANCE RELIEF CORPS ON THE BATTLEFIELD.

VISCOUNT de Flavigney, minister of war, gave us permission to dispose of the Irish wherever we pleased, so we resolved to bring them to Evreux. We arrived there towards the middle of October, and three days after the battle of Pacy-sur-Eure was fought, and the Irish doctors were the only ones left to take care of the sick and wounded. In the meantime, we returned to Tours, and left the Ambulance Relief Corps in charge of Mr. Bourse. We shall not mention the many services rendered by the Irish Ambulance in the other towns and villages of Beauce and Normandy; suffice it to say, that from the time they arrived, until the end of the war, they continually looked after the wants of the sick and wounded; moreover, the Ambulance cost not one penny to our country, for it was supplied with everything from Ireland.

THE STUDENT AND THE BLACK CHARGER.

After the battle of Buchy, Mr. Ryan, a young student of eighteen, was taken prisoner by the

Prussians. He protested, and proved that he belonged to the Irish Ambulance Corps, but all to no purpose; he would not be listened to at all. There was a beautiful black charger standing near by, which belonged to one of the Prussian officers. It just took one moment, and that Irish lad was in the saddle and away. Volley after volley was fired at him, happily, without effect. When about a mile off, to his surprise and consternation, four soldiers stepped out in front of him, and called on him to halt. With his revolver, he lays one soldier dead, wounds another, and finally escapes from the other two, and comes galloping in triumph into Honfleur, carried by the magnificent black charger of the Prussian officer.

CHAPTER IV.

Visit to England by Messrs. De Flavigney, Serurier, Ricord and Demarquay.

WE must acknowledge that the English people have given us much during the late war, and it is certain that a very large number of them sympathized with us. It was their interest to do so. It was to the advantage of England that the French military power should be maintained. This was seen after the war, when France having no voice, Russia abrogated the treaty of Paris, notwithstanding England's protestations.

Messrs. de Flavigney, Serurier, Ricord and Demarquay, were charged with the task of thanking the English people for what assistance they gave us during the war. Receptions and dinners were given to the delegates, officially, by the authorities. To these receptions and dinners, was also invited the Prussian ambassador, and M. de Flavigney in his remarks, had common sense enough not to show his astonishment at such lack of good taste, to say the least.

We received much sympathy from many of the English people, but when we come to consider the aid given officially by England, we must say we did not admire it. How they manœuvred in order not to break the neutrality laws! If we received an orange from one, some one else would send three to the Prussians.

Let us pass over and see how Ireland treated us. Ireland did not bother herself about neutrality laws. What did she care whether Bismarck was displeased or not? She was our true friend; she, like France, had no love for Prussia.

CHAPTER V.

FROM PARIS TO LONDON. AUGUST 15TH.

VISCOUNT de Flavigney, Mrs. Dr. Panouse, Mrs. Pitrey and her two daughters, set out from Paris on the 14th. On the following day, Mr. and Mrs. Ferdinand de Lesseps, Dr. Rufz and daughter, and myself, said good-bye to our friends. When we arrived at Calais, the boat was ready to take us off, and after a few minutes we all went on board. The sea is always very rough here, which fact, together with the smallness of the boat, and poor accommodation, makes the voyage very unenjoyable. Almost every passenger was sea-sick. At last the white cliffs of Dover could be seen in the distance, and shortly afterwards we landed. Then it was that our trouble commenced. Trunks, bags, and valises were opened for inspection, and if not opened immediately, locks and straps were broken and lids were smashed by the officials. After all the fussing, nothing of a contraband nature was found amongst our effects. It was just 6 p. m. when we arrived in London. We directed our steps to the House of Parliament to see Mr. J. P. Smith. On entering a large hall, we were directed to the House of Commons by a big policeman, who told us Mr. Smith was not present, and another one said he was. We waited and waited, but no Mr. Smith came to us. Finally, a messenger approached and asked for our card. Five minutes later we were introduced to Mr. Smith, Secretary of the House. Not long after we had the pleasure of shaking hands with the real Mr. Smith, who brought us off to have tea with him. Afterwards we went to the House of Commons, and there listened to a very dull speech by one of the M. P.'s.

CHAPTER VI.

FROM LONDON TO HOLYHEAD.
AUGUST 16TH.

THE preceding evening, the whole party decided to take the 7.30 a. m. train for Holyhead. One of the gentlemen left strict orders with one of the waiters of the hotel to wake him up at 6 a. m. He went to bed early, and slept as sound as a top, until he awoke, and then reaching out for his vest, he pulled out his watch and found it was 6.45 a. m. It took him just three minutes to make his toilet. Down to the dining room he ran, ordered a cup of tea, and in the meantime he gave the waiter a good sound tongue thrashing in broken English, for having failed to wake him up in time. He paid his bill in French gold, handing over to the proprietor one hundred francs ($20 or £5), and of course expected to get back English money in change. But seeing his hurry to get away, the proprietor put on an addition to his bill, and to all the questions he asked, and signs he made to recover his money, he answered not a word, neither English nor French. Not having many minutes to spare, he gave up all hope of getting back his change. So he jumped into a cab, and off he went to the railroad station, in the very worst of humor. From such hospitality may the Lord deliver us.

Calling a man to take charge of his trunk, he went to get his ticket. While awaiting his turn at the ticket-office, the man and the trunk had disappeared, and where to find them he could not tell. He looked up and down, in and out, here and there, but all to no purpose. Finally after getting seated in the train, his lost friends made their appearance, and then the train moved out. From London to Chester the country is very level and uniform. On our arrival at Holyhead we immediately went on board the magnificent steamer which carries the mail to Kingstown. To our great surprise, we found Mr. E. Lesage and Mr. McCann waiting for us. These gentlemen brought us to the dining-room and entertained us most agreeably. We enjoyed our voyage very much. The sea, which is very rough at times, was as calm as a lake. To give an idea of its calmness, one of the ladies inquired what time the boat would leave for Kingstown, although we were already twenty minutes at sea. After four hours out, the mountains of Ireland became visible, and not very long after Kingstown could be plainly seen. Mr. Lesage pointed out the high chimney of a lead manufacturing establishment, built, it would seem, on the top of the mountain; the reason of its being built so high, was because formerly the arsenic which came from the lead used to poison all the cattle for miles around. The chimney is swept every three years, and about two thousand pounds worth of arsenic is gathered each time.

CHAPTER VII.

ARRIVAL AT KINGSTOWN. AUGUST 16TH.

IT was said that 20,000 persons came to welcome the French delegation to Kingstown. The delegation was composed of the following named persons: Count de Flavigney, president of the society, Viscountess de la Panouse, Viscountess de Pitray, Mr. de Lesseps, Dr. Rufz de Lavison, Miss Rufz de Lavison, his daughter, Viscount O'Neill de Tyrone, Mr. Henry O'Neill, lieutenant in the army, Mr. D. Couchin, Mr. and Mrs. Galishon, Captain de Cantenson, Mr. O'Scanlon, reporter during the war for an Irish paper, and Mr. Alfred Duquet.

It was just 5.30 p. m. when the boat touched the quay at Kingstown. We were met at the landing by Messrs. John Martin, M. Sullivan, T. D. Sullivan, M. Lombard, M. McCabe-Fay, J. J. Kennedy, E. McMahon, P. Falty, J. Twohig, Alderman McCann, Dr. O'Leary and J. McMahon, from Dublin; Mr. J. O'Reilly, H. O'Rorke, J. Crostwaite, J. Sullivan, S. Brasel, W. Fitzgerald, and J. O'Reilly, from Kingstown.

After the usual presentations, Mr. O'Reilly read the following address:—

"To Count de Flavigney, president of the Society, and to the distinguished personages who accompany him: The geographical situation of Kingstown gives to its corporation the honor of being the first to extend to the illustrious sons and daughters of France the cordial welcome of the Irish nation. We recognize in you the indefatigable champions of humanity; and, while we remember that charity consecrates your visit amongst us, we cannot forget that the history of France and that of Ireland are intimately connected, and that they teach us lessons of mutual love and veneration."

M. de Flavigney replied:—

"*Gentlemen of the Committee:* Allow me to thank you for the manner you have received us, and for the honor you have bestowed upon us, in presenting us with this address in the name of your beautiful city of Kingstown. Let me tell you how happy we are to be amongst you. (Applause.) In placing our feet on Irish soil, it seems to me that we are again breathing the air of France; that we are back again amongst our friends and families. It is impossible to convey to you a just idea of the sentiments that are now uppermost in our minds. I have tried to reply in your own language, and if I have not been well understood, I know I can rely upon your indulgence. All my words come from my heart. (Renewed applause).

CHAPTER VIII.

FROM KINGSTOWN TO DUBLIN.
AUGUST 16TH.

AFTER the address, a passage was made, and we were taken to open carriages which were in waiting to bring us to Dublin. It was just 6 p. m. when we started for Dublin. The road from Kingstown was a beautiful sight. The French and Irish flags were carried in procession. It was grand! Such joy! such enthusiasm! We never witnessed anything like it before. Everywhere along the whole route, men, women and children joined in the same cry of, "Hurrah for the French!" "Long live MacMahon!" "God save Ireland!" "France for ever!" There never was in my opinion, such a reception given to any living king as we received. M. de Lesseps, who travelled extensively, and saw so many people, told us he was completely surprised at the extraordinary ovation, the like of which he never witnessed in all his life. Some of the papers in speaking of the immense crowd who came to Dublin that day, put the number at 600,000, although that seems a little exaggerated; yet, we are certain there were not less than 400,000 who came to do honor to the sons and daughters of France.

CHAPTER IX.

BREAKFAST AT MR. LOMBARD'S; GRAND
MEETING AND BANQUET. AUGUST 17TH.

WE were magnificently installed at the Shelbourne by the Irish Ambulance Committee, the members of which bore all the expense themselves. On the morning of the 17th, at 10 a. m., we had breakfast with Mr. James Lombard, president of the Committee; he and his daughter, Mrs. Murphy, entertained us in grand style. We must mention here, that the ladies who came to represent France, did it with a most charming grace. Mr. de Flavigney was placed at table between the Lord Mayor and his wife. We sat beside a priest who spoke French well.

After breakfast, we went to the meeting in the rotunda. This meeting was called by the Committee, who gave in their final report and discharged the Ambulance Relief Corps. The approaches to the great hall were completely filled with people, and as to the hall itself, it was more than filled, it was packed. At 3 p. m., the Lord Mayor and Mr. de Flavigney and his companions, and the Ambulance Committee entered the hall amidst the cheers of the populace; the Lord Mayor took the chair. Mr.

Lesage then presented to Mr. de Flavigney, an address in which he expressed how Ireland regretted very much her inability to give any more than a poor offering to her "sister in distress."

"When you return to your country, say that you have found a friend and an ally; say you have found a people who are for France, and for France only, because they cannot forget what France has done for them 'in the days of old.' The sun of victory will shine again as brightly as ever over the banner of France; and Europe will render homage to her once more, as the true champion of religion, of civilization and of liberty."

Mr. de Flavigney replied :—

"*My Lord Mayor and Gentlemen:* After the enthusiastic demonstration made yesterday in honor of France, by the people of your beautiful city, we are very happy to unanimously express to you our profound gratitude; you have done much to lessen the misery which the late war necessarily brought with it, and you have done it in a most generous manner; you would have done more if the neutrality laws were not opposed to your desires, but we appreciate your good intentions, and our gratitude is just the same. Other nations have sent us aid in various ways, but Ireland alone has sent hers with an affectionate peculiarity all her own, and you alone have inscribed on your banner, 'Franco-Irish Ambulance.'

"Certainly, it is not necessary to tell you, that

your surgeons took more care of the French than of the Prussian soldiers; this again shows your sympathy for France. This organized charity is the most noble conquest of modern times. The Red Cross, first thought of by Mr. Dunant, and sanctioned by the convention of Geneva, has become the emblem of charity in the military world. And now let me say, if we have come here to thank you in the name of our society, our Government, also, will offer you some public testimony of its gratitude. All those who have taken part in sending aid to us, and in caring for our poor wounded soldiers, will very soon receive the decoration of the legion of honor."

THE O'NEILLS.

Mr. A. M. Sullivan then presented Viscount O'Neill of Tyrone, with a beautifully bound volume entitled, " The Destinies and Fortunes of the Chiefs of Tyrone and Tirconnell."

Mr. O'Neill was visibly moved, and thanked Mr. Sullivan for his beautiful gift. The family of O'Neill is one of the most ancient, and one of the most illustrious in all Ireland. The O'Neills have reigned in Ireland without interruption for more than five hundred years.

Nial of the nine hostages was the most famous of pagan monarchs. All his energies appear to have been devoted to his hostile expeditions against Albion, Britain, and Gaul. It was probably in his last descent upon Gaul, that a little boy, named Patrick, was, together with his sisters Dorerca and Lupita, first carried among other captives to Ireland. Holy prize! Thrice happy expedition! for this little boy was afterwards no other than the famous St. Patrick, the great apostle of Erin.

Among the most illustrious of the O'Neills, we may mention Shane O'Neill and his nephew Hugh O'Neill. Shane was once offered a title by Elizabeth, but he treated her with scorn and said, that as Ulster had belonged to his ancestors, so it now belonged to him, and having won it by the sword, by the sword he was resolved to keep it.

Hugh O'Neill of Tyrone, waged war with Elizabeth for seven years, which cost her an enormous amount of men and money. He was so much feared by England that his name became a terror to her soldiers, and at the words "Tyrone's coming," they would oftentimes retreat, and wait many days before giving battle. At last, poor man, he had to fly from his beloved land. He went to Rome, and there died in 1616.

The present Viscount O'Neill is a direct desendant of Hugh O'Neill of Tyrone.

OWEN ROE O'NEILL.

On June 18, 1642, Owen Roe O'Neill, nephew of Hugh O'Neill of Tyrone, came from Spain, and took the field against the English. He met the foe at a place called Benburb. It was in the afternoon of a fine day in June he gave the order to advance. The whole Irish army rushed upon the English with pike and sword and carried all before them, leaving over 2000 of them dead upon the field. The Irish loss was less than 100.

Owen Roe O'Neill died in 1649. He was considered to be one of Ireland's great commanders, and his death was mourned for a long time throughout the whole island.

Mr. Lesage then read the following letter from Rt. Rev. Mgr. Dupanloup, Bishop of Orleans:—

"I have just received your kind invitation to be present at the banquet of the Irish Ambulance Committee. I am extremely thankful for this invitation and I regret very much my inability to be with you. I say I regret it very much, because then I would have an opportunity not only to thank you personally for your friendship, but also to thank all Ireland for what it has done for us during the late war.

"Gentlemen, I cannot express to you how grateful I feel for your friendship, so firm and sincere. Heretofore there were many ties which united France with Catholic Ireland, but now, Gentlemen, they are united for ever, as St. Paul says, 'ad cor vivendum et commoriendum.'

"Gentlemen, believe me, etc.,
✠ Felix, Bishop of Orleans, France."

A letter from Marshal MacMahon was then read by Mr. J. Martin.

VERSAILLES, FRANCE,
Headquarters of the Army,
August 6*th*, 1871.

"*Gentlemen:*—I feel very grateful for the compliments you have addressed to me, and for the kind invitation to be present at the banquet to be given to the president of the French Ambulance Society. Kindly express my thanks to all those who would be pleased to see me there, for, at present, I cannot leave Versailles, which I regret as much as yourselves.

"Gentlemen, I have the honor, etc.,

P. MACMAHON."

Mr. McCabe-Fay, secretary, then read the entire report of the committee. Finally, the meeting adjourned *sine die*, with three cheers for France. After the meeting, we met Dr. Baxter, head surgeon of the Ambulance Corps; we shook hands, and remained together a few minutes, then bade each other good-bye, the crowd still cheering for France.

THE WORKINGMEN.

If the French workingmen could only take a trip over to Ireland, they would see their Irish brothers listen religiously to the advice of honest men in whom they have placed their confidence. They would see, also, a laudable tolerance of the opinions of their opponents. Indeed, the Irish workingmen ask nothing but what is just, viz: the amelioration of their condition, brought about by peaceful means, a political renovation approved by equity and common sense; whilst in France, what do many of the workingmen want? It matters very little to many of them what form of government exists, provided they get enough to eat, and plenty of time to enjoy themselves. There are men in Paris to-day, who go to work Thursday, Friday and Saturday, and spend the rest of the week in idleness, and these men earn from five and six, to ten francs a day. Their poor wives and children have to be supported by public charity, because the men spend their earnings foolishly. It is pleasant, however, to look upon the other side of the picture; to think of the many men who are honest and upright, sober and industrious, who, putting their trust in God, support their families as best they can.

THE REPUBLIC.

Our country to-day should be ruled by an iron hand. We do not mean one iron hand, for we dread the singular number. Let us be conservative. Our form of government now is republican, then let us uphold the Republic. If those at the head of the government do not please us, let us, by our votes, compel them to step down and out. If, on the other

IRELAND AND FRANCE. 35

hand, we were ruled by a bad king, a revolution only could remove him, and of revolutions we have had enough. Those in authority should enforce the laws, no matter who breaks them, otherwise our Republic will be a republic in name only.

NO HOME RULE FOR IRELAND.

As to Ireland, we cannot understand how it is, that England approves Home Rule for Italy, Hungary, Holland, Belgium, Egypt, Greece, Canada, and Australia, and yet, she will not consent to give it to Ireland.

THE BANQUET.

On the evening of the 17th the banquet took place. It was given in the hall of the exposition, which was richly decorated with evergreens, flowers and flags. At one end of the hall there was a large table somewhat raised above the others, and it was at this table the Lord Mayor sat. At his right was seated Mrs. de la Panouse, Count de Flavigney, Mr. de Lesseps, Mr. Lombard, Mrs. Petry, Mrs. Galishon, Miss de Lavison, the duke of Feltre, and Mr. A. M. Sullivan. On his left, the Lord Mayor's wife, Viscount O'Neill, Dr. Rufz de Lavison, Mr. John Martin, Mr. Maguire, Mr. D. Cochin, Mr. Galishon, Mr. O'Scanlon, Mr. Henry O'Neill, Mr. de Cantenson, Mr. de la Chaise, and Mr. Alfred Duquet. Around the other tables were seated three hundred of the most illustrious persons

BANQUET AT DUBLIN.

in the nation. The gallery was filled with ladies and gentlemen who paid to listen to the speeches. Behind the table of honor, a splendid orchestra played national airs.

Now the toasts commence. Listen! The Lord Mayor proposes the health of Queen Victoria. Then arose the storm of hisses, about which the English press talked so much. The French were in no way responsible for such a demonstration. The same thing would have happened if the banquet were given in honor of the Great-Mogul.

The Lord Mayor then drank to the health of the Lord Lieutenant, whom he regarded as the best sportsman in the three kingdoms. These brilliant qualities are not very much admired by the Irish, and the toast was a failure. The Lord Mayor was defeated twice, it is true, but the third time his victory was complete. "To the Representatives of France," was received with tremendous cheers, with joy and enthusiasm which cannot be described. Here is what he said:—

"I propose a toast to our distinguished visitors, the representatives of the French nation. I feel great difficulty in proposing a toast of such importance, for when I consider the high rank, the personal merit, and the charitable sentiments of those men and women who have come amongst us, my embarrassment increases the more. Here is Count de Flavigney, president of the ambulance society, separated from his family, away from home, in order to serve his country and take care of the poor wounded soldiers. We have also here a man with royal Irish blood in his veins, Viscount O'Neill of Tyrone, the grandson of an illustrious Irishman. Here also is the Duke of Feltre. He, too, is of Irish origin, and there is Mr. de Lesseps, who built the great canal which unites two seas."

Count de Flavigney then arose, and made a speech in English, as follows :—

"*My Lord, Ladies and Gentlemen:* The splendid reception given to us by the people of Kingstown, and by the people of Dublin to-day, prove beyond doubt, your love and affection for us. This reception has filled our hearts with joy, because we know it was given, not so much for us personally, as for our beloved country, France, and it will be a great consolation for her to know that she has such an ardent and true friend in this little green Isle of yours. (Applause.)

"At the meeting this morning, the report of the services of your ambulance was read; but the great services which it has rendered to the poor soldiers have been but too modestly represented.

"We were shut up in Paris during the war, but we have been informed about what you have done. To give an example, Dr. Baxter, the head surgeon, not only saved the life of the soldiers, but on one occasion he saved the lives of the inhabitants of a whole city. One day a Prussian soldier was wounded, the general heard of it, and swore he would destroy the city immediately. Dr. Baxter obtained a delay until he extracted the ball from the wound. The ball proved to be shot from a Prussian gun. The general was satisfied.

" Provisions sent by Ireland came in great abundance, and the poor as well as the rich contributed. I again repeat that your ambulance did us a great service. We hope you shall never want the assistance of France. You are happy and prosperous now [cries of no! no! no!]; but if you ever find yourselves in like circumstances, you can depend upon us." (Cheers).

Viscount O'Neil of Tyrone, then proposed " Ireland" as the next toast. Mr. John Martin replied. He said :—

" Ireland and France love each other, because of a certain similitude in their qualities, and when I say qualities, I mean faults also, because a nation without faults, would be a queer and strange nation. France is still the most powerful, as well as the most Christian nation, notwithstanding the many reverses she has suffered. Political circumstances have changed the genius of Ireland, but the spirit of both nations is the same, and sooner or later, they will give each other a helping hand.

" The demonstration given yesterday by the Irish people shows their love, their respect and their inalienable friendship for the representatives of France. Our friends know well that a public demonstration is not complete in which neither police nor soldiers take part, but they know also, that Ireland is not her own mistress; that she owns neither soldiers nor police. There was nothing official in yesterday's reception. It was the expression of heartfelt sympathy of the Irish people."

At the conclusion of this speech, Mr. A. M. Sullivan arose and proposed, "To France, our Benefactor."

"*My Lord Mayor, My Lords, Ladies and Gentlemen:* My colleagues of the committee have imposed a heavy task on me, not forgetting that night and day during this week, I took my humble part in the reception which was to be given to the nation our benefactor. But no matter what has been my labor in this work, it was only a labor of love for me, and when I want to express the sentiments of love and affection, which Ireland has for France, it is not necessary for me to be prepared. (Applause.)

"My Lords, Ladies and Gentlemen: He who would speak of France as she deserves, should retrace the history of everything that is great and glorious in the civilization of the world. If you take France from the map of the world, you at the same time bind the human race in the chains of slavery. And as sometimes you see clouds rise, and after a while gradually fade away, leaving behind those beautiful shades of blue, so we see France at first rise from the midst of savage grandeur, then by degrees traverse through the different phases of the feudal times, of chivalry, of romance and of song.

"In the time of Charlemagne, France occupied the first place in Europe, teaching the nations sitting at her feet the fine arts, civilization, religion and liberty. (Applause.)

"Read the history of France, and see what the chisel of the sculptor, the brush of the artist, and the pen of the poet have done for letters and art during the days such as those of the reign of Louis XIV.

"Read the history of France, and you will see that in the revolutionary times, when this great nation suffered under the feudal system, during the hours of her sorrowful agony, she made tyrants tremble on their thrones.

"Read the history of Europe, read it down to our own times, and see what France has done, marching at the head and realizing in our own days the dream of the Pharaohs, the uniting of two seas. I mean what future historians will narrate as the work of five hundred years, the work of Ferdinand de Lesseps. (Great applause.)

"I ask you where is the Prussian; where is the Englishman that could ever cut through an isthmus? But, My Lords, Ladies and Gentlemen, it is not for these reasons that we propose a toast to France. It is not because she is great, glorious, and free. It is not because she is powerful. No! No! If we have given her a magnificent ovation, that

Kings might envy, it is because France has something still greater, something still nobler, than her power, and her glory. It is because, of all the nations, she has been the only generous and disinterested one among them, and she is the only nation, that has drawn the sword to redress the wrongs of the oppressed. (Applause.)

"Whether it was to expel the Turk from Greece or chase the Goths and Vandals from Rome and protect the Vicar of Christ in the Eternal City, or send aid to Ireland in her troubles, or lend a helping-hand to the United States of America in their struggle to be free, France has always taken the leading part.

"Let me tell you, sons and daughters of France, there is no place else where all this is better remembered than in dear old Ireland. (Applause.)

"THE IRISH EXILES.

"My Lords, Ladies and Gentlemen: There is not and there never was, a spectacle so full of tragic grandeur, as the exodus of the flower and nobility of Ireland which gave to France the Clarks, the O'Neills, and the McMahons.

"Tell me of all the national struggles you can think of. Show me the monuments of victories won, from Moscow to Madrid, and tell me what nation can represent such a spectacle of immolation and self-sacrifice, as that which was seen, when the ancestors of the Duke of Feltre and Viscount O'Neill of Tyrone departed forever from the land of their birth? Well might they lament with the poet when he said :—

"Farewell, lovely Erin, the home of my childhood,
    Thy green sunny hills I may ne'er see again;
But my heart will return to the castle and wildwood,
    And ever with Erin will fondly remain.

"No more will I roam through the green fields of Ireland,
    Or pluck the green shamrock that grows in the vale;
But I'll hate the oppressors, who've ruined my sireland,
    And sent me an exile from dear Innisfail.

"Farewell, dearest Erin, now and forever,
    The home where my comrades and true friends do dwell,
My heart, it is breaking to think we must sever,
    Adieu, lovely Erin, forever farewell.

"For the Earls would rather homeless roam
    Where freedom and their God might lead,
Than be the sleekest slaves at home,
    That crouches to the conqueror's heel.
                    (Tremendous applause.)

"Dearly beloved France! In remembrance of these heroes, Ireland presses you to her bosom. To-day you drink the chalice of bitterness, but have faith, have courage! If Europe has forgotten what she owes you; if the nations have turned their backs on you, while the enemy was at your gates; if they have placed themselves, like cowards, behind that word neutrality; no matter! Turn your eyes towards the west, and listen! 'Tis the voice of Ireland, as she strives to break her chains: '*O God! that these hands were free to help my benefactor!*' (Tremendous applause.)

"Animated by these sentiments, I ask of this assembly of Irish ladies and gentlemen to stand up, and drink the toast, '*God save France!*'"

Three ringing cheers were then given for France.

It was in the midst of the general emotion that Mr. de Lesseps arose and replied to the very eloquent speech of Mr. Sullivan.

"*My Lords, Ladies and Gentlemen:* I remember once to have read of a certain countryman of yours, who, being invited to a great banquet given in his honor, was, of course, expected to make a speech. He spent a great part of his life striving to gain her liberty, and at the same time he was loaded down with honors by the king and his ministers.

Being in a very delicate position, every one was anxious to hear what he had to say. At last his turn came, he got up very slowly from his chair, bowed gracefully to the audience and said, 'Thanks.' Knowing that the audience was surprised and disappointed, he turned towards his neighbor, and whispered loud enough to be heard by everyone, 'Have I said too much?' This, of course, brought down the house.

"Ladies and Gentlemen, I know you would not be pleased with me, if I should follow his example. Permit me to remark, I am very glad to be able to say a few words in reply to the very eloquent speech to which we are just after listening.

"There has always been sentiments of esteem and affection existing between France and Ireland. From my childhood I have been accustomed to love Ireland, and the reason I loved it was, because I have always heard my father and mother speak well of Ireland. From time immemorial, under every form of government, this love of France for Ireland has existed, and has been many times expressed by the French press, no matter what else were the opinions of these organs. And after what we witnessed yesterday, we can testify to the love which Ireland has for France."

Many other toasts were drunk, and amongst them was one I cannot pass over in silence. It was to the French ladies; to which the Duke of Feltre replied in a happy speech, and at midnight the banquet terminated.

CHAPTER X.

ADDRESS BY THE MUNICIPALITY. SIGHT-SEEING THROUGH THE CITY. DINNER WITH THE LORD LIEUTENANT. AUGUST 18TH.

ON the 18th at noon, the members of the municipality of the city of Dublin, came to present an address to the French delegates. The costume of the members was certainly very remarkable. They put one in mind of the men of some great eastern potentate, with their robes, their swords, and their golden chains. Being introduced into the drawing-room of the hotel, they were received by Mr. Flavigney and his companions. The Lord Mayor, after shaking hands with us, read the following address :—

"*Count de Flavigney:* We, the Lord Mayor and Aldermen of the city of Dublin, wish you and your honorable colleagues a cordial welcome to our city. In doing so, we express the sentiments of the Irish people. We feel great satisfaction to know that the efforts made by Ireland in aid of the sick and wounded soldiers in the late war, have been so much appreciated by the French people."

This was the third address that Mr. Flavigney received, and we must say they were beautiful, not only in the manner in which they were gotten up, but more especially on account of the sentiments of love and affection which they expressed. The president of the committee brought them home to France, and keeps them as precious souvenirs of our visit to Ireland.

Mr. de Flavigney replied that it was a great honor to receive such an address. He thanked Ireland for the manner in which he and his companions had been received. It was also his desire that France would sooner or later strike a blow for Ireland. He said that he was now far advanced in years, and that he could not hope to be of use very long, but that he had a son, now Mayor of one of the cities of France, who knew of all the services the Irish ambulance had rendered during the war, and who would always remember the warm reception given to his countrymen by the people of Dublin.

At one p. m., the members of the committee came for us to go visit the principal places in the city. We were first taken to the old parliament house, very near which is the statue of the great O'Connell. Then we were taken to the park, which contains ten thousand acres of the best of land. It was here that the famous meeting took place, which was dispersed by the police. Mr. P. J. Smith was addressing the people from the steps of the Wellington monument, when the police, who are governed by

Orangemen, made an onslaught on the unoffending people, who numbered fifty thousand, many of whom were killed and wounded. Then we made a pilgrimage to the tomb of O'Connell; it is a very imposing one. A marble sarcophagus contains the casket, which can be seen through a glass cover. Over the door, written in gothic letters, are the last words of the illustrious liberator, "*I leave my body to Ireland, my heart to Rome, and my soul to God.*"

We cannot help relating an incident which happened during the same day. Two French gentlemen made up their minds to do the city all by themselves. One of them proposed to have their pictures taken while in Dublin. In passing along, they saw just what they wanted, a photographer's. They went in, and immediately commenced to make their business known to the proprietor, but all to no purpose. They could not make themselves understood. One of the gentlemen thought he could speak English very well, but when he strove to tell that they wanted their pictures taken he failed completely. He made signs, he made faces, and strove in every possible way to convey his ideas to the photographer, but the poor man gave it up. Then calling to his wife, he said in French, "Felicie, come here a minute. There are two fools here, whom I cannot understand. Try, and find out what they want if you can." "Oh, you are French!" exclaimed our two friends. "You should have told us that at first." The photographer was dumbfounded for a moment. He then commenced to excuse himself for what he had said. He told how he used to trade in oil, but business being dull he bought this little shop in Dublin, and came over here to live.

We then paid a visit to Mr. Smith, M. P., who entertained us most royally, after which we went to dine with the Lord Lieutenant. It was decided that we should accept the invitation, for whatever might be our particular opinions, it would be an insult to refuse to go.

The residence of the Lord Lieutenant is in Phoenix Park, and like most English castles, is not very imposing. At 8 p. m. the French delegates went to the castle, and were received by the chamberlain, the Lord Lieutenant being not at home.

Lord Spenser is very rich. He has in his possession some of the very finest plate, which came down to him from the famous Marlborough. Here is the Menu :—

   Vice Regal Lodge. August 18th, 1871.
Potage Jardiniere, a la Xavier,
  Tarbots Bouillis, Sauces homard,
    Fause Tourte, a l'Anglais,
      Filets de Samon, a la Bernice,
 Cassolettes garnies de Moelle, a l'Espaguolle,
Filets de Poulets, a la Royale,
    Salmis de Coqs de Brugre, au Chasseur,

Dindonneaux, a la Macedonie, Jambons, au Madere,
    Hauches de Venaison Roties,
            Selle de Moutons Roties,
    Cailles Roties Bardees Leverauts,
Petis Pois, a la Francaise,   Chants aus Anglais,
        Flau de Peches, a la modern, .
    Profitrolles au chocolat, a la Vanille,
Chrochauts glaces, a la Cylan, Gateau a l'Elizabeth.

Now as the menu is known, we shall give the names of those who partook of it. The Lord Lieutenant and his wife, the French consul and his wife, Lord Kildare, Lord Meath, Lord Monck and their wives, Mr. Burk, Sir Henry Havrelock and his wife, Colonel Corrigan, the President of the Medical Faculty, the President of the Faculty of Surgeons, Count Jarnac, Lord Sandhurst and wife, Captain Bing, Count de Flavigney, Mesdames de a Panouse and Petry, Mr. and Mrs. de Lesseps, Viscount O'Neill of Tyrone, Mr. Henry O'Neill, Mr. and Mrs. Galishon, the Duke of Feltre, Mr. Alfred Duquet, Mr. de Cantenson, Mr. Dennis Cochin, Mr. Maguire, Mr. O'Scanlan, Mr. H. Thompson, Mr. C. Boyle and Captain Briggs.

During the banquet, the band of the 70th Regiment of Infantry played several choice pieces.

After the dessert, Lord Spenser stood up, and when all the rest had followed his example, he took his glass, raised it, and with deliberation said simply "To the Queen." The band immediately struck up

"God save the Queen," and when the last notes had died away, we all sat down again. The ladies, then following the English custom, retired to the drawing-room, leaving the gentlemen all alone. This custom is said to date back far into the ages. Gossip has it, that after the dessert, and when the wines had been indulged in, at many of the banquets given then, the male portion of the gathering generally used to fall off their seats and roll under the table. This spectacle, of course, displeased the ladies very much, so they made up their minds to get out of the way before the accident occurred. But why keep up the custom, since no such accidents occur nowadays? At 6 p. m., we joined the ladies in the drawing-room, where special artists were engaged to entertain us until midnight. The Lord Lieutenant did all in his power to make it pleasant for us, and he succeeded admirably.

CHAPTER XI.

Excursion to the County Wicklow.
August 19th and 20th.

ALL the members of the French delegation set out, under the direction of Mr. O'Sullivan, on an excursion to the charming county Wicklow. We went by rail to Bray, a beautiful summer resort. After leaving Bray, we proceeded as far as the long glen, through which the river Dargle flows; the length of the famous glen is about a mile, and the height of some of the enclosing walls of rocks exceeds three hundred feet. The view of the glen from above is most beautiful; here is a combination of rugged rock and foliage of every tint and form, with the Dargle leaping and foaming beneath. One of the best places, for a good view of the glen, is at the "Lover's Leap." Then we visited the waterfall at Lord Powerscourt. The fall is about three hundred feet, and when the volume of water is large, it descends from rock to rock, with a rush and a roar that is very impressive. Afterwards, we proceeded to the Vartry Waterworks. It is from here that Dublin is supplied with water, through a very ingenious system of siphons, the like of which we have never seen before. After lunch at Vartry,

POWERSCOURT WATERFALL.

we were driven towards Glendalough. In the villages, through which we passed, the French flag was everywhere to be seen, and the people were assembled in crowds shouting, "Hurrah for France! God save Ireland! God save France!" We wish we could have all our countrymen see and hear the demonstrations that were made in our behalf. It was really touching; and notwithstanding all the fatigue which we endured during our visit to Ireland, we can never think of that country and its chivalrous people without sentiments of emotion.

After Mass, the next morning, we continued our journey on towards the Seven Churches

AT GLENDALOUGH.

Many and curious are the traditions current regarding the founder of a seat of learning in this lonely wilderness. The founder, St. Kevin, was born in the year 498, was baptized by St. Colman, was educated by Patrocus and ordained by Bishop Lugid. He was contemporary with St. Columkille. He led a hermit's life, in a place called Luagen Duach, since called Glendalough. The erection of seven churches is ascribed to St. Kevin there. A city sprang up, and a seminary founded, from whence was sent forth many exemplary men, whose sanctity and learning diffused around the Western world the light of the Gospel. St. Kevin died in 618, after leading a holy life, at the age of 120 years.

IRELAND AND FRANCE.

From the Seven Churches, to "The Meeting of the Waters," is about ten miles. The beautiful vale of Avoca, in which the waters of two rivers meet, is celebrated in song by one of Ireland's gifted sons, Thomas Moore.

"There is not in the wide world a valley so sweet,
As the vale in whose bosom the bright waters meet.
Oh! the last rays of feeling and life must depart,
Ere the bloom of that valley shall fade from my heart.

Yet it was not that nature had shed o'er the scene
Her purest of crystal and brightest of green;
'Twas not her soft magic of streamlet or hill,
Oh, no! it was something more exquisite still.

'Twas that friends, the beloved of my bosom, were near,
Who made every dear scene of enchantment more dear,
And who felt how the best charms of Nature improve,
When we see them reflected from looks that we love.

Sweet vale of Avoca! how calm could I rest
In thy bosom of shade with the friends I love best,
Where the storms that we feel in this cold world should cease,
And our hearts like thy waters, be mingled in peace."

Cars were in waiting to bring us up the mountain side. We were met by the inhabitants of the town, with bands of music. We were saluted with "Vive la France!" "Hurrah for France!" Arriving at last at the top of the mountain, we were conducted to the orphan asylum, presided over by Rev. Father Fox. We regret to be obliged to repeat the same thing over and over again, but let us say with Molière: "Je dis toujours la meme chose, parseque c'est toujours la meme chose; si ce n'etait pas toujours la meme chose, je ne dirais pas toujours la meme chose."

The people of the surrounding country were there, with music playing, banners flying, and drums beating, and the boys drawn up in line to receive us. The Rev. Father then showed us to the dining-room, where we partook of his hospitality. Mr. Smith made a speech in French, to which the Director of the establishment replied in eloquent words, saying in part, that he was more honored that day, by our visit, than if the Lord Lieutenant had come to see them. Having spent some time in looking over the different apartments of the establishment, we said au revoir to the good Father and his companions, and then returned to Dublin. That day one of our party, Mr. de Lesseps, was called home to Paris on urgent business.

CHAPTER XII.

OUR VISIT TO CORK AND MALLOW.
AUGUST 21ST AND 22ND.

FROM Dublin to Cork is 165 miles; the route passes through a very pleasant stretch of country. At many places good views are obtained of the picturesque mountain ranges. It was on the morning of the 21st we set out for Cork, with Messrs. John Martin and Mr. O'Sullivan. All the people were there to see us off. "Bon voyage for Cork!" "Good-bye!" "Three cheers for Count de Flavigney!" "Hurrah for the French!" were some of the parting salutations. At every station along the road a great number of people gathered to see us. At Marlborough, where we were presented with an address, there was a great demonstration. The address, which was read by the Mayor, was very artistically enscribed on parchment, and tied with green ribbons. M. de Flavigney responded. Oh, what joy! What enthusiasm!

At Thurles the enthusiasm was redoubled; but it was at Limerick Junction that we got the greatest reception yet. The inhabitants of Tipperary turned out in their thousands. Seldom has any one seen such manifestations of joy. The name of M. de Flavigney,

O'Neill of Tyrone, the French ladies, the French Republic, were cheered to the echo. The bands played the Marseillaise. The Marseillaise, that beautiful hymn so prostituted (by the sang-impur de Belleville) that we are almost ashamed of it, yet we like it very much indeed.

Very soon after passing Limerick Junction, we obtained a splendid view of the famous Galtee mountains in the distance. A few small stations, and then we arrived at Mallow, where the crowds of people were exceedingly large. The bands were playing national airs, whilst the French and Irish flags were flying in the breeze on all sides. We were then conducted to our hotel, passing under several triumphal arches on the way. The magistrate of the town was delighted to present the address, to which Mr. de Flavigney immediately replied. A great crowd assembled under the window of our hotel and repeatedly called for the French delegation; we all went out on the veranda, where our president addressed the people again. The band played once more, and wondering at such manifestations of friendship, each one retired to his room completely tired out. The following morning we were escorted from the hotel to the railroad station amidst the the same manifestations of joy; then

WE STARTED FOR BLARNEY.

The following is taken from the Cork *Herald*, of August 23d, 1871:—

Entry into Cork.

"Yesterday will be written in letters of gold in the history of Cork. Never have the walls of the old city resounded with such cries of joy as those that were heard yesterday. It is simply impossible to describe the manner in which France was complimented, and the chivalrous reception which was given to the delegation. No words can express the enthusiasm which dominated the reception.

"It is only three months since the Lord Lieutenant of her Majesty in Ireland made his official entry into Cork, surrounded by soldiers. There was not one cry of joy to salute him; there was not one establishment decorated in his honor; there were no flags displayed; in one word there was no enthusiasm. Yesterday a simple delegation arrived to thank Ireland in the name of France. What a difference between this reception and that of the Lord, who came with all the pomp of royalty. All the millions of England could not purchase for him such an ovation."

The foregoing article is here inserted to show that a more than royal welcome was given to the French by the inhabitants of Cork.

The Lord Mayor and the members of the city government met us at the town of Blarney, five miles from Cork. Here is the famous castle, built by Cormac McCarthy in the fifteenth century. Tradition has it, that a certain stone in the castle has been endowed with the curious power of conferring on those who kiss it a remarkable flow of eloquence. The poet, speaking of the stone, says:—

"There is a stone there
That whosoever kisses,
Oh! he never misses
To grow eloquent.

A clever spouter
He'll sure turn out, or
An out and outer,
To be let alone.

Don't hope to hinder him,
Or to bewilder him;
Sure he's a pilgrim
From the Blarney Stone."

Our time being limited, we did not kiss the Blarney Stone, so we took carriages here, and after driving rapidly for some time along the "beautiful banks of the Lee," we were met by hundreds of people who came out of the city to get a good look at the French. About a mile from Cork were assembled the members of the city corporation; the societies of the different parishes with banners; viz., St. Finbar, St. Mary, St. Denis, St. Louis, St. Luke, St. Patrick, and many others.

After having taken our places in the different barouches, the procession commenced to march, whilst the crowd at the same time augmented in numbers. As was mentioned once before, we are at a loss to find words to convey to our readers the impressions which the demonstration produced on our minds. The enthusiasm was simply indescribable. The French and Irish flags were waving from every house. The French and Irish colors were worn by every man, woman and child. All, or nearly all, carried green branches in their hands.

It was just 12.15 p. m. when we entered the city. In front of the Queen's College (a Government Institution) a tremendous ovation took place, as we heard repeated, "O'Neill of Tyrone! O'Neill of Tyrone!" Then came the cry, "God save France! Hurrah for the French Republic! Down with Bismarck!" etc. As the procession advanced through South Main street, the enthusiasm became more pronounced. We shall never forget how beautiful the women looked, as they smiled and bowed to us, with their rosy cheeks and laughing eyes. From South Main street we turned into St. Patrick street, where the statue of Father Matthew stands; from there we turned down the Grand Parade, and then on to the South Mall. At last we arrived at the Imperial Hotel amidst thunderous applause.

The Lord Mayor met us in the drawing-room of the hotel. An address was presented by one of the members of the city government. Many thanks were given to us for having condescended to visit the capital of the South. Reminding us that the sympathies of Ireland were with France, the address terminated with these words: "We offer you the hospitality of our city, and we wish that your visit may be very enjoyable, and we regret exceedingly that your engagement elsewhere prevents us from keeping you very long amongst us."

Our President replied in excellent English:—

"*My Lord, and Gentlemen of the City Corporation:* The address which you have had the kindness to present to us, expresses in eloquent terms the sentiments which, from time immemorial, have united Ireland and France. (Hear! hear!)

"There is something mysterious, something very sympathetic in the affection which these two nations feel for each other. It is something as strong as family relationship; it is something greater than the relation which exists between kings and their governments. (Hear! hear!)

"The only man capable of expressing these sentiments is Marshal MacMahon. But, unfortunately, he is not here. He regrets very much that he could not come with us, to thank you for what you have done for his beloved country. He is not the least gift which Ireland bestowed on France. In our late distress, he has rendered to us untold services. He has been the preserver of society, and the saviour of our country. He is a great man, and we all know that he is Irish. As he has not been able to accompany us, we have brought other Frenchmen of Irish origin. Here is Count O'Neill of Tyrone, who bears a great and respected name in this country. Here, also, is the Duke de Feltre, whose grandfather was an Irishman, and a Marshal of France.

"Gentlemen: Allow me to tell you of the great services which your nation has rendered to us during the late war. Excuse me, Gentlemen, but I am unable to suppress the feelings of emotion which arise in my breast, when I think of them. The Irish soldiers, who were with our troops, conducted themselves like heroes. Captain Leader, for example, at the battle of Orleans, placed himself at the head of his company, and fought the Prussians until he had used up all his ammunition. (Applause.) After which he saluted the enemy, and then the French Army, and afterwards retired to the rear. Many Irishmen have been decorated for their bravery during the war. The city of Cork was the first to send money and provisions to our society. And Ireland sent to us a magnificent ambulance for the wounded soldiers. Two distinguished physicians, Drs. Baxter and Maguire, rendered great services to the poor wounded men. The Ambulance Corps was constantly and abundantly supplied from this country. And when other nations abandoned us, Ireland came to our aid in every way she could, although obliged to observe the laws of neutrality.

"Gentlemen: We come here to return to you and all Ireland, our heartfelt thanks for your kindness. I must say you have received us most royally, and it will be a great consolation to us, when we return home, to be able to tell our countrymen, with what sentiments of love and affection we were received by the people of Ireland." (Great applause.)

Then an address was presented by the Workingmen's Club:—

"To Count de Flavigney, and to the distinguished persons who accompany him: Sons and daughters of chivalrous France. The noble Count de Flavigney has perfectly expressed our sentiments, representing France and Ireland as two sisters. We are proud to declare, that if we have acted as we have done, it is with the view to bind together still more firmly with the bonds of love and affection the two countries, France and Ireland. Unfortunately, the profound and cordial sympathy of Ireland towards France, was expressed only feebly, because we could do no more. Oh! if Ireland was only permitted to join your brave soldiers to hurl back your enemy! In the hope that generous France will believe our good intentions, we wish long life to the French Republic."

The Lord Mayor then announced that a deputation from the town of Youghall, was ready to present an address to our president. The address was read by Mr. Ronayne, to which M. de Flavigney responded.

Mr. John Martin, being called by the people, he went to one of the windows and made a speech, which was interrupted several times by frequent bursts of applause. He said in substance: "France has always been the friend of Ireland, and the

French people have a very good right to love Ireland." He then complimented the people of Cork, for the admirable reception which they gave to the delegation. He hoped that before very long Ireland would become her own mistress, and a nation once again, and then she could dispose of her army and navy as she pleased. (We must mention here that Mr. John Martin is a Protestant, very well liked by the Catholic clergy, because of his liberal views.)

At 2 p. m., we were conducted to the steamer City of Cork, where we had luncheon. By that time the crowds had again gathered in full force, everywhere along the banks of the river. All the boats were packed with human beings, who continued cheering, waving their handkerchiefs, and clapping their hands. We then sailed down the river, and as we passed by the cruisers Lord Warden and Mersy, we were saluted in grand style. It is difficult to overpraise the beauty of the river from Cork to the Cove, now called Queenstown.

Here is a stream ever varying in its course and outline, of ample breadth, yet not too broad to prevent distinct recognition of the objects on its banks. Water of a color and purity of the sea. Lofty barriers on either side, covered with rich woods, and intermingled with green park-like fields, and shining villas. At last Queenstown came into view, that famous town, from which so many of Ireland's sons and daughters embark for the land of the free.

The people almost went wild on our arrival, and cheer after cheer was given for the French. The ships in the harbor saluted as the City of Cork sailed down between them. A visit was then paid to the battle-ship Northumberland which is said to be the largest in the world, except the Great-Eastern. Captain Gibbons received us very graciously on board. During our visit we noticed the band played St. Patrick's Day, The Marseillaise, and God save Ireland. Then we were transferred to our own boat which sailed over to a little creek called Ashgrove, where dinner was served, after which the speech-making commenced.

Mr. Murphy endeavored to respond to the toast, "Her Majesty the Queen," but failed completely. His audience would not listen to him, so he was obliged to sit down. The Lord Mayor, Mr. de Flavigney, Mr. John Martin, and Mr. O'Sullivan also made speeches.

A celebrated orator (whose name we don't remember), being pressed to say something, when his turn came, refused at first, but afterwards consented, as his name was called several times. He said:—

"*Ladies and Gentlemen:* You appear to desire very much that I should make an interesting discourse to you on this occasion. I have the same desire myself. Unfortunately, we do not receive French men and women, every day at our table, and this, with the fact of my being able to shake hands with them to-day, has so overjoyed me, that I have drank, not exactly too much, but in fact I have celebrated the event in a very extraordinary manner for me. I therefore ask your permission to keep silent, for my tongue can utter nothing at this moment, without blundering, except these words, 'Hurrah for France! Hurrah for Ireland! God save France! God save Ireland!'"

This last speech "took down the house."

At 8 p. m. the boat returned to Cork, where we were met by a great crowd carrying torches. They conducted us to the Imperial hotel, all the streets leading to it being packed with young and old, cheering and asking to see us once more. We all appeared at the different windows, and our president again addressed the people, thanking them for the grand demonstration that was made in our behalf. Mr. John Martin, again made a ringing speech, the last words of which were, "Long live the French Republic! God save Ireland!"

The Duke of Feltre, and M. O'Neill of Tyrone, being called, addressed a few words to the people in like manner. Then Mr. O'Sullivan, having thanked the inhabitants of Cork for the magnificent demonstration given in honor of the French delegation, he recommended them to go home, and very soon after, the streets were deserted. Thus terminated, according to one of the evening papers, the grandest ovation ever given to any one in the city of Cork.

CHAPTER XIII.

FROM CORK TO GLENGARRIFFE.
AUGUST 23RD.

THE morning of the 23rd we bade good-bye to the people of Cork, twenty-one guns being fired as we pulled out of the station. Very soon we arrived at Macroom, where we were met by the priest of the parish, and his flock, who gave us a hearty welcome. After the indispensable address, they brought us along the streets under triumphal arches, to the castle, with its old square towers. We had not time to go through all its apartments, yet, what we saw of it, was charming. After saying adieu, away we went. The usual road to Glengarriffe is to proceed to Bantry by the north one. In turning to the left we entered the Garra valley, by the river Toon with its zig-zag courses. Above the valley are rocky ledges. After passing the ruined tower of Dundericke, we journeyed through a succession of steep and rugged glens, until we reached the little lake of Inchigeelagh. Here were assembled the inhabitants of the surrounding country, carrying green branches, cheering, and clapping their hands. During the demonstration we have seen women cry with joy, as we passed along. Some will say, no doubt, that we are exaggerating. We have not in the least exaggerated anything, for we have all been witnesses to the extraordinary outbursts of popular feeling, not only here, but in every town and village, through which we passed.

Mr. Murphy, of Bantry, had ordered a nice lunch for us, on the shore of the beautiful Gougane-Barra. This mountain lake, the source of the Lee, is surrounded on three sides by very lofty cliffs. Near the centre of the lake is an island, on which lived St. Finbar. Here are the ruins of the monastery, the chapel, etc. There is a holy well near-by, to which pilgrimages are made from many parts of Ireland.

J. J. Callanan describes the island in his beautiful poem, as follows:—

There is a green island in lone Gougane-Barra,
Whence Allu of songs rushes forth like an arrow
In deep-valleyed Desmond, a thousand wild fountains
Come down to that lake from their home in the mountains.
There grows the wild ash; and a time-stricken willow
Looks chidingly down on the mirth of the billow,
As, like some gay child that sad monitor scorning,
It lightly laughs back to the laugh of the morning.

And its zone of dark hills—Oh, to see them all
 brightening,
When the tempest flings out his red banner of
 lightning,
And the waters come down, 'mid the thunder's deep
 rattle,
Like clans from the hills at the voice of the battle;
And brightly the fire-crested billows are gleaming,
And wildly from Malloc the eagles are screaming
O, where is the dwelling, in valley or highland,
So meet for a bard as that lone little island?

How oft, when summer sun rested on Clara,
And lit the blue headland of sullen Ivara,
Have I sought thee, sweet spot, from my home by
 the ocean,
And trod all thy wilds, with a minstrel's devotion.
And thought on the bards, who, oft gathering to-
 gether,
In the cleft of thy rocks, and the depth of thy heather,
Dwelt far from the Saxon's dark bondage and
 slaughter
As they raised their last song by the rush of thy
 water.

Last bard of the free! were it mine to inherit
The fire of thy harp, and the wing of thy spirit,
With the wrongs, which, like thee, to my own land
 have bound me,
Did your mantle of song throw its radiance around
 me.

Yet, yet on those bold cliffs, might Liberty rally,
And abroad, send her cry o'er the sleep of each valley.
But rouse thee, vain dreamer! no fond fancy cherish,
Thy vision of Freedom, in bloodshed must perish.

I soon shall be gone, though my name may be spoken,
When Erin awakes, and her fetters are broken.
Some minstrel will come, in the summer eve's gleaming,
When freedom's young light on his spirit is beaming,
To bend o'er my grave with a tear of emotion,
Where calm Avonbuee seeks the kisses of ocean,
And a wild wreath to plant from the banks of that river
O'er the heart and the harp that are silent forever.

At 1 p. m. we shook hands with our amiable friends, and proceeded on our way towards Glengariff. Very soon we entered the pass of Keimaneigh, one of the grandest defiles in Ireland. Precipitous walls of rock rise on both sides, clothed with mosses, ferns and shrubs. And as we descend by the river, Bantry Bay opens out before us.

THE FRENCH INVASION.

"Viva la, the French are coming,
Viva la, our friends are true.
Viva la, the French are coming;
What will the poor yeomen do?

It was here the French, under General Hoche, intended to land in 1796, and strike a blow for Ireland. France and England being at war, messengers were sent from Ireland to the French Directory, asking their assistance to cast off the hated yoke of England and establish a republic in its stead. About the middle of September, General Hoche promised the expedition should sail for Ireland. It appears that everything was ready about that time, but from many difficulties made by the department of the Marine, it was not until the fifteenth of December that the armament sailed from Brest, which consisted of seventeen sail of the line, thirteen frigates, and fifteen transports, making in all forty-five sail, and having on board an army of eighteen thousand men. The squadron set sail the fifteenth with the Commander-in-Chief of the Army, and the Admiral on board the same frigate, which was afterwards admitted to be a grave mistake on their part.

ENGLAND IS SAVED BY THE WINDS.

The army never landed. For six days the remains of the fleet lay tossing within sight of the Irish shore, after having been four times dispersed by terrible storms. Out of forty-five sail, they were reduced to sixteen, with only six thousand fitting men on board; even with this number of men, had a landing been hazarded, there would be every chance of success, if we consider the state of the country at the time. But General Grouchy, who was in command, hesitated; the flag-ship, with Hoche, being blown out to sea. After a day's cruising in the bay, a terrible gale set in from shore, and then a landing was out of the question. Again the ships were scattered over the waters. Nothing was left then, but to return as best one could to France.

General Hoche himself, was obliged, after a fruitless visit to Bantry Bay, to make his way back to France, not having seen a single ship of his fleet the whole time. Thus terminated the expedition which gave such a shock to England. The memory of this invasion is still kept green in the hearts of the young generation of this part of Ireland. It may be asked, what would have happened, if Hoche had landed with his fine army at Bantry, amongst those stalworth sons of the South?

Another surprise awaited us at this famous Bantry Bay. As we advanced over the mountain, the day was drawing to a close. After sunset, little by little night came on, and the darkness could almost be felt. But lo! as if some fairy hand had wielded a magic wand, all was light. The mountains as far as we could see, the villages all around us were in a blaze. Bonfires here and there, and everywhere. We could not describe the effect which the sudden illumination produced on each and every one of us. We shall certainly never forget it.

CHAPTER XIV.

From Glengarriffe to Killarney.
August 24th.

AT last we arrived at Glengarriffe hotel, where Mr. John Cullinane, of Bantry, entertained us.

THE MARCH OF O'SULLIVAN.

It was from Glengarriffe that the famous O'Sullivan marched, in December, 1602, to O'Rorke's castle, in the County Leitrim, with a thousand men. It was considered at the time to be one of the greatest achievements of the age. He went right through the heart of the country, which was held by the English. The foe surrounded him on all sides. He was greatly incumbered by the women and children, the sick and the aged, whom he had to protect. He crossed a large river in boats made of horses' skins. Whenever he encountered the English, he always came out victorious. In one engagement he slew the commander, and marched on in triumph to his friend's home in Leitrim.

" I wandered at eve by Glengarriffe's sweet water,
   Half in the shade and half in the moon,
And thought of the time when the Sacsanach slaughter
   Reddened the night and darkened the noon;

Mo nuar! mo nuar! mo nuar! * I said,—
 When I think, in this valley and sky,
 Where true lovers and poets should sigh,
Of the time when its chieftain O'Sullivan fled.

Then my mind went along with O'Sullivan marching
 Over Musk'ry's moors and Ormond's plain,
His *curachs* the waves of the Shannon o'erarching,
 And his pathway mile-marked with the slain:
Mo nuar! mo nuar! mo nuar! I said,—
 Yet 'twas better far from you to go,
 And to battle with torrent and foe,
Than linger as slaves where your sweet waters spread.

But my fancy burst on, like a clan o'er the border,
 To times that seemed almost at hand,
When grasping her banner old Erin's *Lamh Laidir*
 Alone shall rule over the rescued land:
O baotho! O baotho! O baotho! † I said,—
 Be our marching as steady and strong,
 And freemen our valleys shall throng,
When the last of our foemen is vanquished and fled!

Here it rained all night long, so much so that the little rivulets became roaring torrents. At 6 a. m., all were ready to set out. As we drove along the shore of Bantry Bay, the view was as beautiful,

---

* *Alas.* † *O fine.*

if not more so, than any on the Mediterranean. As we ascended the side of the mountain, the wind commenced to blow a gale, and the rain came down in torrents. Our umbrellas were turned inside-out. Our hats would not stay on our heads. Our words were cut in two, and respiration became difficult. At last, we arrived near the summit, where there was a little shelter. Here a tunnel is cut through the mountain, somewhat like that of St. Gervais at Chamony. Arriving at the other side of the mountain we had a magnificent view of the valley lying before us. Our difficulties were not over yet awhile, for the storm still continued. Down the mountain side we go at a lively pace; the cars rock from side to side, but our steeds are sure-footed, and our drivers are skillful handlers of the reins. Arriving at Kenmare, the people came to welcome us, headed by the town officials, one of whom read a beautifully illuminated address. After lunch a visit was paid to the Church and convent school, which is conducted by the Sisters of Mercy. In the school we were entertained by the children, who sang for us the French hymn:—

"Allons enfants de la Patrie,
Le jour de gloire est arrivé.
Contre nous de la tyrannie
L'etandard sanglant est levé," etc.

CHAPTER XV.

KILLARNEY. AUGUST 25TH.

LEAVING Kenmare behind we passed through the windy Gap. A full view is here obtained of Killarney's mountains: the Reeks, the Gap of Dunloe, the purple mountains. Here and there are craggy cliffs, projecting rocks, and desolate glens. What wild grandeur of wood and water, glen and mountain? By-and-by, however, the scene changes. The lakes! the lakes!

> " By Killarney's lakes and fells,
>   Emerald isles and winding bays,
> Mountain paths and woodland dells
>   Memory ever fondly stays.
>
> Beauteous nature loves all lands,
>   Beauty wanders everywhere,
> Footprints leaves on many strands,
>   But her home is surely there.
>
> Angels fold their wings and rest
>   In that Eden of the West,
> Beauty's home, Killarney—
>   Ever fair Killarney.

Innisfallen's ruined shine
  May suggest a passing sigh,
But man's faith can ne'er decline
  Such God's wonders floating by
    Castle Lough and Glena Bay,
    Mountains Torc and Eagle's Nest.

Still at Mucross you must pray,
  Tho' the monks are now at rest;
Angels wonder not that man, there
  Would fain prolong life's span,
    Beauty's home, Killarney—
    Ever fair Killarney."

The inhabitants of Killarney turned out to welcome the delegates in true Irish style. The salutations that greeted our ears were: "Long live the French Republic!" "Long live MacMahon!" "Hurrah for the French." An address was presented by Mr. O'Donohoe, M. P., to which Mr. de Flavigney replied. We were then driven to the Lake Hotel, which was beautifully decorated with French and Irish colors. All around the hotel was lighted up with Chinese lanterns and red fire, resembling very much the fairyland we read of in story books; and every one, even to the servants, wore the tricolor.

FRANCE WAS BEATEN BECAUSE SHE WAS NOT PREPARED FOR WAR.

We were up bright and early the following morning to take a look around. Just outside the hotel we met Mr. McGaven, with whom we very gladly took a walk in the bright sunshine, in that beautiful spot of earth. During our conversation the subject of the late war was introduced. Mr. McGaven wanted to know why France was beaten. We replied that it was because France was unprepared for war, while Germany was well prepared. Ever since 1866 it became more and more evident that France and Prussia would come to blows sooner or later.

Some time ago we visited Prussia, and while there several people told us that they intended to annex Alsace and Lorraine; and when we told in Paris what we heard, every one laughed at us. The Prussians, they said, will not dare to put their feet on French soil. If they do, we'll rise in our thousands and wipe them off the face of the earth. Every one knows how Prussia was preparing for the conflict, night and day, since '66, while in France every thing military was completely ignored. There was a lot of speech-making in the Chamber of Deputies about our commerce, our industries, and our public instruction, etc., but not one word was said, not one voice was raised to arouse the nation to the real state of affairs. The war came as predicted, and we were found unprepared for it, and that is the reason why France was beaten.

On our coming back to the hotel, the barouches, decorated in the national colors, were waiting to bring us to the lakes.

It is only by a row on the lakes, says Black, that the loveliness of their scenery can be fully realized. The changing contours of the mountains, the luxuriant foliage clothing the winding shores of the lakes and the lesser hills adjoining them, the numerous islets that dot their surface, are in this way seen to much better advantage than on land; and, indeed, no one can be said to have really visited the Lakes of Killarney who has not enjoyed the pleasure of a row over them.

Proceeding towards the lakes, in company with Monsignor Moriarty, Bishop of the Diocese, and Lord Castleross, we passed the castle, now in ruins and clad with ivy. The Abbey of Mucross is a picturesque and beautiful ruin. It was founded in 1340 by the Franciscans. The cloisters are in the form of a piazza, surrounding a courtyard, having in its centre a magnificent yew tree of very great age.

The boats were ready to take us over the lakes, as we came to the shore, and now pursuing our course, we passed one or two islands on our way to Innisfallen. Before landing we came to O'Sullivan's Cascade, which consists of three falls: the first one falls twenty feet, straight down into a basin, then it rushes down into a second basin, from which it rolls over into the lowest chamber of the fall. Innisfallen is celebrated for its exceedingly great beauty, but more especially for its ancient abbey, whose ruins are scattered about the island. The "Annals of Innisfallen" are considered very valuable at the present time; the original copy being written over six hundred years ago in this old abbey. The "Annals" contains parts of the Old Testament, and a universal history, down to St. Patrick, and the history of Ireland, to the end of the 13th century. The island is about twenty acres in all, and from it can be had the most lovely views. Speaking of it, Moore says:—

"Sweet Innisfallen, fare thee well,
   May calm and sunshine long be thine,
How fair thou art, let others tell,
   While but to feel how fair, be mine.

Sweet Innisfallen, long shall dwell
   In Memory's dream that sunny smile,
Which o'er thee on that evening fell
   When first I saw thy fairy isle."

The Upper Lake is about two and one-half miles long, and though it is the smallest of the three, it is the most beautiful of them all. No doubt, this is owing to its nearness to the mountains, which rise abruptly from the water's edge. The wild grandeur of this lake, he writes, strikes the observer, on first beholding it, with feelings of awe and admiration.

The Eagle's Nest rears its head 1,700 feet. It is a rugged mass of rock, and the grey eagles still have their eyries here. The echo from this and the surrounding rocks is remarkable, especially in calm weather. A bugle call we may hear repeated nearly a dozen times, and answered from mountain to mountain, sometimes loud and without interval, and then fainter and fainter, and after a sudden pause, again arising as if from some distant glen, then insensibly dying away. The Middle Lake contains about 680 acres, and the Lower Lake has about 5,000 acres, or five miles long and three miles broad, and there are about thirty islands in it.

CHAPTER XVI.

KILLARNEY TO DUBLIN. AUGUST 26TH.

THE following day we took our departure from this charming town, after bidding adieu to its good people, who showered on us many acts of kindness. Before we boarded the train, some one decorated our trunks with the tricolor, which was appreciated by us very much, as then they were easily distinguished from the other pieces of luggage. All our effects were looked after by Antonio, the servant of the Duke de Feltre, so nothing went astray.

At every station along the way, from Killarney to Dublin, large crowds were waiting to meet us. A beautiful address was presented to us at Kildare, and at 5 p. m. our train pulled into the Broadstone Station, Dublin.

ORANGE BIGOTRY.

Whilst the Irish papers rejoiced every day, at the grand demonstrations made in our behalf, the Orange sheets showed their spleen by headings, such as: "The Queen Insulted," "The Laws Broken," "Shall the Police let the Ignorant People break the Sabbath, by these Demonstrations on Sunday?"

"The Scandal of it all," "It cannot be Allowed." We noticed, also, some of the English papers, viz.: The *Times*, the *Pall-Mall Gazette*, and the *Daily News*, making the same lamentations and shedding the same crocodile tears. It appears that *l'Opinion Nationale*, which did so much towards uniting Italy with Germany, cannot see the use of an Irish nation, yet Ireland was our ally, whilst Italy and Germany were our enemies.

THE PRESIDENT CHARMED THE PEOPLE.

Count de Flavigney, President of the French delegation, fulfilled his mission splendidly. A man of much experience, calm, serious, and full of reserve, who spoke the English language fluently, and while he charmed the Irish people, he never said a word which could give offense to the English government.

THE FORESTERS.

We almost forgot to mention that the Foresters, a benevolent society, presented an address to us. The delegates came, in their green regalia, to the Shelbourn, and expressed their loyalty and attachment to the great French nation, in very eloquent words.

DINNER AT THE MANSION HOUSE.

The Lord Mayor gave a dinner at the Mansion House, on the 26th inst. Mrs. Lavison and Mrs. de la Panouse being indisposed, could not attend.

Mrs. Pitray had to bear all the honors, and she did so with admirable grace. The Lord Mayor sat at the head of the table, with Mrs. Pitray to his right, also Mr. John Grey, M. P., and Mr. Lavison; and on his left were Miss Smollen, Count O'Neill of Tyrone, and Mrs. Murphy, etc. My next neighbor was Miss Campbell, eldest daughter of the Lord Mayor; then came Count de Flavigney, and the wife of the Lord Mayor, and the Duke de Feltre.

When dinner was nearly over, the Lord Mayor proposed the health of the Queen; then an old gentleman, who looked like a judge, sang "God save the Queen;" every one standing during the singing of the royal hymn. Then he drank to the health of Mr. de Flavigney, and again the old gentleman commenced to sing the Marseillaise. Our President replied in part as follows:—

"*My Lord Mayor, Ladies and Gentlemen:* In proposing my health, at so distinguished a reunion, and in terms so flattering, you confer on me a great favor.

"I am very happy to be able to profit of this last occasion, to thank Ireland once again for the magnificent reception which she has given to her French guests. From the time of our arrival, the officials, who represent the sovereign, have honored us in every possible way which lay in their power. My Lord Mayor, you yourself, and all the members of your corporation, have each and every one shown us the kindest attention. The cities, towns and villages, through which we passed, have received us in a manner that kings might envy. The outburst of affection, from young and old of this land, for my beloved country, was indeed very touching. It is very consoling for France to be thus assured, in the midst of her trials, that here, at least, she has a people who sympathize with her. My Lord, believe me, we shall never forget the happy days that we passed amongst you. That France, also, will always remember what Ireland has done for her. We came here to pay a debt of gratitude, but instead of that, we have contracted a new one, which, please God, we may one day be able to pay back a hundred-fold." (Applause.)

Count O'Neill of Tyrone, on the invitation of the Lord Mayor, read the following poem in French, which he had translated from Davis.

LA BRIGADE IRLANDAISE.

La Veille de la Bataille.

" Reunis sous la tente, ils boivent. . . . Cependant
Le comte de Thomond, de leur mess président,
Se lève, verre en main et droit comme une lance :
' Camarades, dit-il, buvons au roi de France !'
Rasades et vivats respondent à ce cri,
   Car aux Anglais n'en déplaise,
   Le roi Louis est chéri
   De la brigade irlandaise.

Buvons à Jaques deux ! On boit avec fracas.
A Georges l'electeur ! Et l'on rit aux eclats,
Bonne chance aux beautés que nous avons aimées
Dans le pays des lacs aux rives embaumées !
Que Dieu garde l'Irlande ! Ils pâlissent ; au coeur
   Sans doute un chagrin leur pèse :
   On ne tremble pas de peur
   Dans la brigade irlandaise.

Comme il fait claire ! La lampe est éteinte pourtant ;
Quel tapage ! Sont-ils tous ivres dans le camp ?...
Aux armes ! Du combat c'est l'aube matinale ;
Cent tambours a la fois battent la générale.
Aussitôt de la tente ils se rendent tout droit
   A l'avant-garde française ;
   C'est là sa place de droit
   A la brigade irlandaise.

De ces preux, francs-buveurs, pas un n'a survécu,
Tous ont été tués ; qu' importe ! Ils ont vaincu.
D'autres ont, après eux, combattu pour la France,
Jamais ils n'ont revu leur terre d'espérance.
De Dunkerque à Belgrade, en tous lieux de combats
   Il n'est plaine ni falaise
   Où ne gisent des soldats
   De la brigade irlandaise."

         (Great applause.)

THE IRISH BRIGADE.

The Eve of the Battle.

"The mess-tent is full, and the glasses are set,
And the gallant Count Thomond is president yet;
The vet'ran arose, like an uplifted lance,
Crying—'Comrades, a health to the monarch of France!'
With bumpers and cheers, they have done as he bade,
For King Louis is loved by the Irish Brigade.

A health to King James, and they bent as they quaffed,
Here's to George the Elector, and fiercely they laughed,
Good luck to the girls, we wooed long ago,
Where Shannon, and Barrow, and Blackwater flow;
'God prosper Old Ireland'—you'd think them afraid,
So pale grew the chiefs of the Irish Brigade.

But, surely, that light cannot come from our lamp?
And that noise—'are they all getting drunk in the camp?'
Hurrah! boys, the morning of battle is come,
And the *generale's* beating on many a drum.
So they rush from the revel to join the parade;
For the van is the right of-the Irish Brigade.

They fought as they revelled, fast, fiery, and true,
And, though victors, they left on the field not a few;

And they, who survived, fought and drank as of
  yore,
But the land of their heart's hope they never saw
  more,
For in far foreign fields, from Dunkirk to Belgrade,
Lie the soldiers and chiefs of the Irish Brigade."

Then Mr. John Grey delivered a very stirring address, and at midnight we bade good-bye to the Lord Mayor, thanking him very much for his kind hospitality.

CHAPTER XVII.

Mass at the Jesuits' Church. Departure of the French Delegates. August 27th.

ON the morning of Sunday, August 27th, the French delegation, with a number of distinguished people of the city, took their places in covered carriages, and were driven to the Church of St. Francis Xavier, to hear Mass. The church belongs to the Jesuits. An immense crowd almost blocked the way. The church was packed. About fifty young men, decorated with French and Irish colors, acted as ushers in, and outside of the church. The music was fine, and the sermon, preached by Rev. Father Bannon, S. J., was a masterpiece of eloquence. The subject was, "France, the queen of civilization, will now become once more the sister, the protector of all oppressed nations;" and many of the congregation were moved to tears during its delivery.

THE DEPARTURE.

For several days beforehand, great preparations were made for our departure for home. The railroads made reduction in the price of tickets, and from all parts of the country, great crowds poured into the city. It was said that more than two thousand francs worth of ribbons were sold during that day. We could not believe that the joyous scenes, on our arrival at Dublin and Cork, could be surpassed, but such was the case, for the manifestations were almost indescribable. The people went wild, in fact. It was very remarkable that there was not a policeman to be seen the whole day. The government, no doubt, decided to keep them in-doors, fearing that there might be a conflict between them and the people.

From 2 p. m., the societies, with bands playing and flags flying, bearing the mottos, "God save France!" and "Erin go Bragh!" moved pass the hotel. There were about fifty bands of music. Every one, men, women and children, wore French and Irish colors. Every house was decorated with the French flag. From Dublin to Kingstown was one mass of humanity. And the cry heard, above all others, was "Hurrah for the French," and "Vive la France!" When we arrived at Kingstown, it was 6.45 p. m., and so great was the crowd here that we could not advance, but only very slowly, and on that account we were too late for the boat going to England. We then decided to stop at the hotel, and wait until the following morning. Many of the people thought we had left on the boat, and retired very soon after to their homes.

During all the excitement, not an accident occurred, and not a policeman put in an appearance, yet every thing went off in perfect order. And we must say, that whilst we were in Ireland, we have not seen a person under the influence of liquor, something we cannot say of England.

We almost forgot to mention, that when the carriage, in which Messrs. de Flavigney, Feltre, Lombard and Duquet, came under one of the triumphal arches, a beautifully ornamented cage was dropped into it. On close examination we found the cage contained a dove, which Mrs. de la Panouse carried home to France.

CHAPTER XVIII.

FROM DUBLIN TO LONDON.
AUGUST 28TH.

SEVERAL members of the delegation desired very much to spend another day in Dublin. Messrs. de Lesseps, Henry O'Neill, Chaise, Galishon and Cochin had already departed from Ireland, and on the 28th, Messrs. Lavison, Rufz and Duquet set out for home. At 7 p. m. we took the train for Kingstown, and a few minutes after, we were on board the boat for Holyhead. It was a beautiful morning—the sun was shining brightly, and the sea was as calm as a lake. We admired the beautiful town of Kingstown, and taking a look at the mountains, far away in the distance, we sailed away. But behold you, all of a sudden, everything was shut out from view. It was impossible to see twenty feet ahead, the fog was so thick. All was bustle, then, on the boat—every one was on the *qui vive.* The fog-horn sounded every minute, the watches were doubled, and every precaution taken to prevent accident. After an hour, the fog lifted as quickly as it came, and we were all happy once more. It takes about five hours to cross the Irish Sea, and the shortest passage is via Holyhead.

IRELAND AND FRANCE.

By this route London can be reached in about eleven hours from Dublin. When our boat landed at Holyhead, we shook hands with the Captain, boarded the train immediately, and away we started for London. Arriving at Euston station at 7 p. m., we had just two hours to wait before setting out for Paris. Lunch over, we ordered a cab, and drove to Charing Cross, from which we took our departure. At this station there was one thing which attracted our attention, and which made every one anxious to find out if his pocket-book was still in his possession. In large print was written :

NOTICE.

The public are warned to be aware of pickpockets, who are generally very well dressed. Women, especially, should not be trusted.

CHAPTER XIX.

FROM LONDON TO PARIS.
AUGUST 28TH, 29TH.

IT took the train just two hours to go from London to Dover, and at 11.30 we went on board the steamer, bound for Calais. The moon shone out brightly, and we could see the white cliffs of Dover disappear, little by little, as we sailed away. Very soon Calais was seen in the distance, and we all rejoiced to know that we would be home again, in a very short time. On landing we were prepared to open our trunks and show our passports, but the commissioner, finding out who we were, let us pass without any bother.

The journey from Calais to Paris made very little impression on some of us, for we went to bed in the former, and awoke in the latter city, the following morning, just twenty-four hours since we set out from Dublin.

At 11 a. m. we were at Versailles, with Marshal MacMahon, telling him about the ovation we received, and the enthusiasm with which his name was received in Ireland. We made a little speech, something in this fashion:—

"Marshal, you have had very good reason not to pay a visit to the land of your forefathers, for, judging from the enthusiasm of the people, at the bare mention of your name, we could not tell what might have happened if you had been there yourself. The Irish people would have been transported by an outburst of joy, affection and admiration for you. There would have been a revolution surely. The people would have simply gone wild over you; and you would have been proclaimed king. Marshal, our advice to you is, when you go to Ireland, go at the head of 100,000 men, as the successor of General Hoche."

The Marshal laughed heartily, and seemed to be very well pleased at the reception we got in Ireland, the home of his ancestors.

CHAPTER XX.

Conclusion.

WHAT conclusion must we draw from the splendid reception which rejoiced the hearts of the members of the French delegation? In the first place, it must be borne in mind, that it was France the Irish people intended to honor in our persons. Ireland worships us and, right or wrong, puts her trust in us, hoping that, through us, her deliverance will come some day. She sang once, and who knows but she may sing again,—

> " Viva la, the French are coming,
> Viva la, our friends are true,
> Viva la, the French are coming;
> What will the poor yeomen do? "

THANKS TO IRELAND.

We should be very thankful to Ireland for all the marks of esteem and affection shown to us during the late war. She was the only nation who came to our relief at the time, and we are certain, that if she had Home Rule, the Irish Parliament would have spent the last penny in our behalf, and would have sent us, not an Irish Brigade, but an Irish army.

Until our dying day we shall always remember the names of Messrs. P. J. Smith, O'Sullivan, Lombard, E. Lesage, McCann, McCabe-Fay, and the members for the county Dublin, and in thinking of them, how can we forget Ireland, and the whole Irish people?

THE END.

PARIS, FRANCE,
    Sept. 14*th*, 1871.

CHAPTER XXI.

THE INTERNATIONAL COMMITTEE FOR THE RELIEF OF THE SICK AND WOUNDED IN WAR.

TREATY OF GENEVA FOR THE AMELIORATION OF THE CONDITION OF THE WOUNDED ON THE FIELD OF BATTLE, AUGUST 22ND, 1864.

THE Governments of Belgium, Baden, Denmark, France, Holland, Portugal, Prussia, Saxony, Spain, Wurtemburg, and also the Federal Council of Switzerland, desiring to mitigate as much as possible the terrible evils of war, by giving relief to the wounded soldiers on the battlefield, have concluded a treaty for this purpose, the articles of which are as follows:—

Article 1. Ambulances and military hospitals shall be acknowledged to be neutral, and as such shall be protected and respected by belligerents, so long as any sick or wounded may be therein. Such neutrality shall cease, if the ambulance or hospitals should be held by military force.

Article 2. Persons employed in hospitals and ambulances, comprising the staff for superintendence, medical service, administration, transport of wounded, as well as chaplains, shall participate in the benefit of neutrality while so employed.

Article 3. The persons mentioned in Article 2 may, even after occupation of the enemy, continue to do their duties in the hospital or ambulance, which they may have, or they may return to the corps to which they belong. When these persons shall cease from their labors, they shall be given up by the occupying army to the enemy. And they shall have the right to send a representative to the commander-in-chief of their own armies.

Article 4. As military hospitals are subject to the laws of war, persons on withdrawing from them must take only what is their own private property. On the contrary, ambulances shall retain all their equipments on going away.

Article 5. The inhabitants of the country, who may bring help to the wounded, shall be respected and shall remain free. The generals of the belligerent powers shall inform the inhabitants of the appeal addressed to their humanity. Every house, in which a wounded soldier is, shall be protected. Every one who entertains a wounded soldier in his house shall be exempted from the quartering of troops, and from the payment of any war tax which may be imposed.

Article 6. Sick and wounded soldiers shall be taken care of, no matter to what nation they may belong. Commanders-in-chief shall have the power to deliver immediately to the enemy soldiers who have been wounded in battle. Those who have recovered from their wounds shall be sent back to their own country. Prisoners also may be sent back on condition that they will not bear arms during the war. Evacuations shall be protected by neutrality laws.

Article 7. A distinctive and uniform flag shall be adopted for hospitals, ambulances and evacuations, and on every occasion be accompanied by the national flag. An arm badge shall also be allowed for neutral persons, but the delivery of these badges shall be left to the military authorities. The arm badge and the flag shall bear a red cross, on a white ground.

Article 8. The details of execution of the present convention shall be regulated by the commanders-in-chief of contending armies, according to the instructions of their home governments, and in conformity with the general principles laid down in this convention.

Article 9. The contracting powers have agreed to communicate the doings of the present convention to those governments which have not found it convenient to send plenipotentiaries to the International Convention at Geneva, with an invitation to accede thereto; the protocol is, for that purpose, left open.

Article 10. The present convention shall be ratified, and the ratification shall be exchanged at Berne, in four months, or sooner, if possible.

In witness thereof, the plenipotentiaries have signed the same and have affixed thereto the seal of their arms.

Done at Geneva, the 23rd day of August, 1864.

List of Governments which Adopted the Treaty.

The governments which signed the articles of the convention of Geneva, are as follows:—

1864. Baden, Belgium, Denmark, France, Italy, Netherlands, Spain, Sweden and Norway.
1865. England, Greece, Mecklenburg, Prussia and Turkey.
1866. Austria, Bavaria, Hesse Darmstadt, Portugal, Saxony and Wurtemburg.
1867. Russia.
1868. Pontifical States.
1874. Persia, Roumania and San Salvador.
1875. Montenegro.
1876. Servia.
1879. Argentine Republic, Chili and Bolivia.
1880. Peru.
1882. United States of America.
1884. Bulgaria.
1886. Japan.
1888. Congo Free States, Hungary and Luxemburg.
1894. Venezuela.
1895. Siam.
1896. South African Republic.
1898. Honduras, Nicaragua, Mexico and Brazil.

The Navy.

Articles signed by the Great Powers in 1868, Concerning the Armies on the Sea.

Article 1. The persons mentioned in Article 2 of the convention shall continue to do their duties to the sick and wounded, after the occupation by the enemy. When those persons wish to go away, the commander shall fix the time of their departure. He may delay it for a very short time in case of necessity.

Article 2. Neutralized persons captured by the army of the enemy may have their salaries paid as heretofore by applying to the contending powers.

Article 3. In Articles 1 and 2 of the convention, the name "ambulance" applies to field hospitals and other temporary establishments which follow the troops on the field of battle to receive the sick and wounded.

Article 4. According to the meaning of Article 5 of the convention, about the quartering of troops and the war tax, account only shall be taken of the charity shown by the inhabitants, their zeal and good-will, in taking care of the wounded soldiers.

Article 5. It is agreed, in addition with Article 6 of the convention, that (officers excepted) the wounded captured by the enemy shall be sent back to their own country, after they are cured, on condition of not bearing arms during the war.

Article 6. During and after a battle at sea, all boats which, at their own peril, pick up the shipwrecked sailors, shall be considered neutral until they have reached the hospital ship, or some other neutral ship. The wrecked and wounded thus saved must not bear arms again during the war.

Article 7. The religious, medical and hospital staff of any captured ship are hereby declared neutral, and on leaving the ship may take away all their private property.

Article 8. The aforesaid staff must fulfill their duties in the captured ship, assisting the wounded, etc.; then they may return to their own country.

Article 9. The hospital ships are under martial law as to their stores. The hospital ships belong to the captor, but must not be used for any other purpose during the war. Vessels intended for hospital ships, and which are not armed, shall enjoy the laws of neutrality, both with regard to their stores and staffs.

Article 10. Merchant ships charged with the removal of the sick and wounded are to be considered neutral. The fact of their being visited by the enemy's ships renders the sick and wounded incapable of bearing arms during the war. If a merchant vessel carries a cargo which is not contraband, she is protected by neutrality. The belligerents retain the right to interdict neutralized vessels from all communication, and from any course which they may deem prejudicial to the secrecy of their operations. Commanders-in-chief may neutralize for a time vessels intended for the removal of the sick and wounded.

Article 11. Sick and wounded soldiers and sailors shall be protected and taken care of by their captors, no matter to what country they may belong. Their return to their own country is subject to the provision of Article 6 of the convention, and of the additional Article 5.

Article 12. The flag to be used with the national flag is to be white, with a red cross in the centre. Boats or ships displaying the white flag may claim the benefits of neutrality. The belligerents may exercise any mode of verification which they may deem necessary. Hospital ships shall be distinguished by being painted white outside, with green strake.

Article 13. The hospital ships, which are equipped at the expense of the aid societies, recognized by the governments signing this convention, and which are furnished with a commission from the sovereign, who shall have given express authority for their being fitted out, and with a certificate from the proper naval authority, that they have been placed under his control during their fitting out, and on their final departure, and that they were then appropriated solely to the purpose of their mission, shall be considered neutral, as well as the whole of their staff. They shall be recognized and protected by the belligerents. They shall make themselves known by hoisting, with their national flag, the white flag with a red cross. The distinctive mark of their staff, while performing their duties, shall be an arm badge of the same color.

The outside painting of these hospital ships shall be white with a red strake. These ships shall bear aid to the wounded and wrecked belligerents without distinction of nationality. They must not interfere in any way with the movements of the combatants. During and after the battle they must do their duty at their own risk and peril.

The combatants shall have the right of controlling them and of visiting them; and they will be at liberty to refuse their assistance, or order them to depart, and to detain them if necessary.

The wrecked sailors and soldiers, picked up by these ships, cannot be claimed by either combatant, but they must not fight any more during the continuance of the war.

Article 14. If either of the combatants takes advantage of the benefits of neutrality, in naval battles, with any other view than the interest of the sick and wounded, the other belligerent has the right to suspend the convention treaty. If it be certain that such is the case, notice may be given to said belligerent that the convention is suspended with regard to him during the whole war.

Article 15. The present act shall be drawn up in a single, original copy, which shall be deposited in the archives of the Swiss confederation.

An authentic copy of this act shall be delivered, with an invitation to adhere to it, to each of the signatory powers of the convention of the 22nd of August, 1864, as well as those who have acceded to it.

In faith whereof, the commissioners have drawn up the present additional articles, and have affixed thereto the seals of their arms.

APPENDIX.

MARSHAL MacMAHON,
President of the French Republic, 1873.

I.—PARENTAGE.

PATRICK MAURICE, Count de MacMahon, and Duke of Magenta, who was born on June 13th, 1808, at the Castle of Sully, in France, belonged to the Clare MacMahons, one of the most ancient families in Ireland; their ancestors having been the O'Briens, kings of Munster, of the race of Heber.

The Marshal's grandfather, John-Baptist MacMahon, was a native of Limerick, where he was born in 1715. He went to France to seek the education denied him at home. Having heard that an Irishman of his name had acquired fame as the principal doctor of the Paris Military School, he embraced that profession. Having been admitted to the profession in 1739, he lived until the year 1775, leaving two sons. The eldest, Charles Laurence, fought with Lafayette for American freedom, became a marquis and a chevalier of St. Louis, received on the first restoration, in 1814, the rank of field-marshal, and was named a peer of France in 1827. He died in 1830.

Count de MacMahon, the younger son of John-Baptist MacMahon, and father of the Marshal, became a colonel in the famous regiment of the Hussars of the Guard in 1789. He was among the royalist exiles of the revolution, and afterwards became the intimate friend of Charles X. Though the traditions of the family were royalist, the mother of MacMahon, a great-granddaughter of the famous engineer, Riquet, befriended more than one of the republican exiles in the days of their adversity. When Courtois, of the Legislative Assembly, had to fly, his orphaned daughter found in the Countess de MacMahon a mother and protector. The Count had seventeen children, nine of whom survived. There were four sons. The third, who was destined for such a famous part in the history of France, was born at the Castle of Sully, on the 13th of June, 1808.

At the age of 17 the future Marshal entered the military school of St. Cyr, from which he graduated with high honors in October, 1827. In January, 1830, he was made lieutenant of the Fourth Hussars, and in the following April he went with the Twentieth Regiment to Algiers, with which country France was then at war. For his brilliant conduct in the war he was made a lieutenant in April, 1831, and in the September following, received the cross of Knight of the Legion of

Honor, a rare honor then for so young a soldier. The young MacMahon returned to France, and in 1833 was made adjutant first, and captain afterwards, of the Eighth Cuirassiers. He returned to Algiers in 1836, but was back in Paris in 1838, when he received the unusual honor of promotion in the Order of the Legion of Honor to the class of officer. From 1840 to 1855 young MacMahon served constantly in Algiers. As lieutenant-colonel of the Foreign Legion he was engaged in all the affairs against the Kabyles, from 1842 to 1844, when he was appointed full colonel of the Forty-first Regiment of the line, in the Province of Oran.

II.—General of Brigade.

In 1848 MacMahon was made General of Brigade and obtained command of the Province of Oran. In 1852 he was appointed to the military government of Constantinople, and was promoted to the rank of General of Division. When the Crimean war broke out General MacMahon was at first appointed to the First Corps of the Army of the North.

III.—The Crimean War.

The plan of campaign being changed, however, the General was sent to the Crimea in the middle of 1855. MacMahon arrived just in time for glory. General Pelissier was preparing for the final assault. He gave the most difficult task—the storming, capture and retention of the Malakoff—to the fresh troops which MacMahon brought. "Count upon us, General," said the latter and his officers, when the plan was unfolded to them. When the moment came (September 8th, 1855) the key of Sebastopol fell to their irresistible rush, and was preserved to them by the cool resource of MacMahon, for the first assault was but the beginning of the fight. The assailants had no sooner become possessed of the position than they had to arrange for its defense. Again and again the Russians returned to regain, if they could, the lost ground. But it was due to the admirable disposition of his forces, made on the spot and under fire by MacMahon, that the prize was saved. His arrangements were so complete that he had settled with his second in command what was to be done in case MacMahon and his Second Brigade were blown up. The possibility was not remote—40,000 kilogrammes of powder had been placed in position and electric connections established. MacMahon's engineer lost not a moment in discovering the latter and cutting them. MacMahon had gripped the Malakoff, and would not loose his hold. The capture made the defense of Sebastopol impossible, and though the English had failed to establish themselves under the terrible fire that swept the Redan, the Russians fired the town when night had fallen, and left the ruins to their foes. MacMahon received for his exploit the Grand Cross of the Legion of Honor, was named

Senator of France, and appointed to the command of the reserves.

IV.—MacMahon Created Marshal and Duke of Magenta.

In September, 1858, MacMahon was appointed commander-in-chief of all the land and sea forces in Algeria. Shortly after this the war with Austria broke out. Early in 1859 MacMahon went to Italy. On June 3rd, commanding the Second Corps of the French army, he routed an Austrian corps at Roechetta, and on the following day won the famous battle of Magenta, which gave the Irish hero his dukedom. The Emperor Napoleon III. and the King of Sardinia, with 55,000 men, were stoutly opposed by 75,000 Austrians, and but for the timely arrival on the field of General MacMahon, the allies would have been disastrously defeated. For this splendid victory MacMahon was made marshal. Twenty days after the battle of Magenta the French and Sardinians gained another signal victory over the Austrians, which was achieved mainly by the skill and bravery of MacMahon, and another gallant Irish general, Neill. This ended the war. When peace was proclaimed Marshal MacMahon returned to Paris and was appointed to the command of the Lille Military District.

V.—Franco-Prussian War. MacMahon's Plans not Heeded.

When the Franco-Prussian war broke out in the Summer of 1870, Marshal MacMahon was intrusted with the command of the Second Division of the grand army organized by the Emperor. Marshal Bazaine had control of the other. The Emperor was nominally commander-in-chief, but his presence, instead of inspiring confidence, had only the effect of paralyzing the action of the real chiefs. On August 2nd, the headquarters of the French army being then at Metz, Marshal MacMahon received orders to move in an easterly direction and feel the strength of the enemy. He advanced as far as Woerth with 40,000 men, when he found himself suddenly overwhelmed by 160,000 Prussians, under the Crown Prince of Prussia. MacMahon's corps was separated from the main army, and the Prussians pressed him hard on all sides. The peril to the French was great, and nothing but the most desperate fighting could save them from being utterly crushed by sheer brute force. MacMahon himself was to be seen, when the smoke would partly clear away, in the midst of showers of bullets, fighting like an enraged lion. Once or twice his assaults were so terrible against the Prussian line, that the Crown Prince was obliged to give ground to the French. For 26 hours he kept the saddle; his horse was killed under him, and his chief of staff was shot at his side.

MacMahon finally succeeded in retreating in good order.* His design was to fall back on Paris, where, with the aid of the force already gathered there, and under the control of Trochu, he felt his ability to cope with the invaders. Bazaine, in the meantime, was strong enough to hold Metz, while the provinces could be organizing fresh armies to march to the aid of MacMahon, who, when he felt himself sufficiently strong, was to have marched to the relief of Bazaine. This was MacMahon's plan, but the stupid officials in Paris ordered him to move at once to Bazaine. The Emperor, whose short-sightedness and truculence brought about the unnecessary and awful war, did not interfere one way or the other after the Woerth disaster. MacMahon, in trying to carry out his superiors' orders, was driven towards Sedan, the trap set for the French by Von Moltke, which MacMahon himself had feared, and into which he was urged by the War Directory at Paris. At Sedan, MacMahon again fought with superhuman energy. "To relate what MacMahon did," said a French officer who was present at the battle, " is impossible. Steel, fire, melted metal, explosive balls, and I don't know what other infernal mixtures the Prussians there made use of for the first time, appeared to stream off or rebound from him like hail from a roof. He went to the front seeking death.\'Leave me, my friends,' he said to us all, who sought to prevent him from going forward, 'let me show those kings, those princes, who hide behind masses of men, that a Marshal of France knows how to fight, and when beaten, how to die.'/ And he smiled upon us a sad smile which made us weep and redoubled our rage. Ah, miserable! We kill, we massacre, and the living appear to spring up from the dead, which we heap around us. We climbed a little mountain of dead bodies that we might reckon how long the butchery would last. My sabre, broken and reeking, fell from my hands when I saw what masses we had still to deal with." MacMahon was frightfully wounded, and the entire French army was compelled to surrender. When MacMahon had sufficiently recovered from his wounds, he was confined a prisoner of war at Wiesbaden, where he remained until peace had been signed.

VI.—MacMahon and the Commune.

MacMahon returned to France on the 15th of March, 1871, just in time to take up the most painful duty that ever fell to his lot. The invader had but retired when civil war blazed forth in Paris, and to MacMahon was given the command of the Army of Versailles, hastily assembled together to recapture the capital from the Communists. It was a laborious and a desperate task. The army was established only on the 6th of April. It began operations five days later, and day by day, and night by night it moved on from position to position, fighting incessantly until the 29th of May. Every suburb, every fort, almost every street in Paris had to be recaptured, and ere the work was done, over 7,000 of MacMahon's army had fallen. Before they were finally beaten, the Communists had become incendiaries, and the devastation of Paris was witnessed with exasperation by the leaders of France.

"Soldiers" wrote MacMahon, when the Vendome Monument had been destroyed, "the column of the Vendome has just fallen. The stranger respected it. The Commune of Paris has overthrown it. Men who style themselves Frenchmen have dared to destroy, under the eyes of the Germans who watch us, that witness of the victories of your fathers against combined Europe. Do they hope, these unworthy assailants of the national glory, to blot out the memory of those soldierly virtues of which that monument was the glorious symbol? Soldiers! if the memories which that column recalled to us are no longer graven upon iron, they are still at least living in our hearts, and drawing inspiration from them, we shall be able to give France a new pledge of bravery, devotion and patriotism."

VII.—MacMahon Elected President of the French Republic.

The work of establishing order being accomplished, MacMahon resumed his military duties. The various Royalist parties hoped that he might bring back the lilies of France and the White flag. \ "Desiring to serve France alone," said MacMahon, "I have loyally served every government that has ruled there." He refused a nomination to the Senate, and devoted himself simply to the work of his office as Commander-in-Chief. / But two years later he was compelled, by his sense of duty to France, to accept the office of President of the Republic. Civil war threatened within, and Bismark was meditating an attack from without upon the nation whose recuperative energy had completely upset the calculations of the authors of the brutal peace of Versailles.* He did not accept it without misgiving.

"Gentlemen," said he to the delegates of the National Assembly, who came to offer him the Presidency, "I am not a politician; I am a soldier, and the title you offer me might it not be used profitably to satisfy certain diplomatic susceptibilities? You have among you men of high merit who could much better fill so delicate a position.

---

* NOTE.—France was obliged to pay Prussia $1,500,000,000 and also to cede Alsace and Lorraine.

I can promise to whoever would accept the functions of chief Executive my most absolute devotion, and I will give my services to him without reserve. I think I can be more useful to the country at the head of the army."

He spoke like the loyal soldier of France that he was; and it was just a loyal soldier that France needed, then, to rally all parties to the cause of national strength and national unity. The delegates of the Assembly prevailed, and in their message to the Assembly they told how "it was only with great difficulty that we could overcome the resistance of the Marshal; but we appealed to his sense of duty, to the sacrifices that he had ever shown himself ready to make for his country; and in accepting, he has given once more proof of the ardent patriotism that makes him so dear to the fatherland."

"It is a heavy responsibility," declared MacMahon in his message of acceptance, "but with the help of God, the devotion of our army, which will ever be the army of the law, the support of all good men, we will combine together for the liberation of the territory and the re-establishment of moral order in our country. We will maintain internal peace and the principles upon which society rests. I give you the word of an honest man and a soldier."

MacMahon's accession to the Presidency synchronized with the union of the Royalist parties and the coming together of the Comte de Chambord and the Comte de Paris. Some among them counted upon MacMahon to restore monarchy by a coup-d'etat. But MacMahon's word was the word of an honest man and a soldier, and when he said that the army should ever be the "army of the law" he meant what he said. Having accepted office from the hands of the National Assembly he would be loyal to the National Assembly and execute what it might decree. If the National Assembly called Henry V. to the throne, MacMahon would have submitted and retired. But he would enter into no conspiracy, and he told the friends of the Comte de Chambord that, friend that he was to the House of Bourbon, "were the white flag substituted for the tricolor in the army the 'Chassepots' would go off of themselves."

MacMahon had resisted the invasion of the constitution by Napoleon. If the Bourbons were to come back it should only be through the portals of the constitution. MacMahon was elected for seven years, and he discharged his duties faithfully. And when he quit the Presidency, it was because he refused to dismiss his companions in arms, in 1879, at the orders of a political party. He stepped down, and out without a murmur, still loyal to the voice of France. He retired to the woods at La Forest a poorer man than when he entered the Elysee. He had refused the

125,000 francs a year, that had been voted him for his traveling expenses. Learning that President Grevy was a poor man, and could not provide the Elysee with the necessary services of plate, he offered his own to his successor. They were accepted, and still remain in the Presidential residence as a proof that the second President of the Republic was superior to the greed of office.

From his retirement from the Presidency, in 1879, until his death in October, 1893, MacMahon lived a quiet, peaceful life, undisturbed by the cares of public office. The valiants of the future were his thoughts when other cares had gone. He was offered some dignified office of state, but he declined it, saying: "When a man has been first in his country, he can become nothing less, except it be a soldier on the frontier, facing the enemy."

The End.

Note.—The translator is indebted to the courtesy of the Editor *Irish World*, N. Y., for permission to include in this volume, the foregoing sketch of Marshal MacMahon, second President of the French Republic.

www.ingramcontent.com/pod-product-compliance
Lightning Source LLC
Chambersburg PA
CBHW031348160426
43196CB00007B/778